George Eliot

THE PROFILES IN LITERATURE SERIES

GENERAL EDITOR : B. C. SOUTHAM, M.A. B.LITT. (OXON.)
*Formerly Department of English, Westfield College,
University of London*

Volumes in this series include

George Eliot

by Ian Adam

Associate Professor in English,
University of Calgary, Alberta

LONDON

ROUTLEDGE & KEGAN PAUL

NEW YORK: HUMANITIES PRESS

First published 1969
by Routledge & Kegan Paul Ltd
Broadway House, 68-74 Carter Lane
London E.C.4
Printed in Great Britain
by Northumberland Press Ltd
Gateshead
© Ian Adam 1969

SBN 7100 6736 4 (c)
SBN 7100 6735 6 (p)

Th ~ofiles in Literature Series

This series is designed to provide the student of literature
and the general reader with a brief and helpful introduction to the major novelists and prose writers in English,
American and foreign literature.

Each volume will provide an account of an individual
author's writing career and works, through a series of carefully chosen extracts illustrating the major aspects of the
author's art. These extracts are accompanied by commen-
tary and analysis, drawing attention to particular features
of the style and treatment. There is no pretence, of course,
that a study of extracts can give a sense of the works as a
whole, but this selective approach enables the reader to
focus his attention upon specific features, and to be informed in his approach by experienced critics and scholars
who are contributing to the series.

The volumes will provide a particularly helpful and
practical form of introduction to writers whose works
are extensive or which present special problems for the
modern reader, who can then proceed with a sense of his
bearings and an informed eye for the writer's art.

An important feature of these books is the extensive reference list of the author's works and the descriptive list
of the most useful biographies, commentaries and critical
studies.

B.C.S.

Contents

CONTENTS

George Eliot—her life and works

George Eliot (whose real name was Mary Ann Evans) is very much a writer of ordinary human experience, whose works emphasize commonplace characters such as rural clergymen, peasants, villagers, or provincial businessmen, or commonplace situations of work, marriage, or family life, or the combination of these. Such emphases provide one reason (among several) why she is often described as a 'realistic' novelist, for one feature of realism in literature is the choice of the normal over the exceptional, the ordinary over the sensational in subject-matter. And while we must qualify the notion of George Eliot as a realist when we consider her *techniques* in different novels, especially the symbolic techniques of the later works, this realism of subject-matter remains a much more constant feature. Yet though her subject-matter may be ordinary, the significance derived from it is not. The reason, of course, lies in her far from ordinary mind, not only in its gifts of wit, observation and sympathy, which are shared with other major novelists, but also in its lucid and energetic intelligence: a gift much more her own. As a result she does more than vividly and sympathetically render her material: she also demonstrates its complexity and importance. George Eliot sees tragedy where others would see a failed marriage, or a complex social organization where others would see a simple village, and she shows why the marriage is tragic, how the village is complex. Her imagination is obviously one which has been formed by sympathetic experience with other human beings, but it has also been formed by intellectual experience which can provide the deep insights of thought. It is perhaps this fusion of intellectual range and depth with a deep feeling for others which Henry James had in mind when he spoke of her as a 'philosophic' novelist—an accurate description if we put the emphasis equally on both words.

The reconciliation of intellectual and emotional needs which we sense achieved in the works was not easily achieved in the life. She was born in 1819, in a rural environment in the midlands. Her childhood shows a deep affection for home, countryside, and family, especially for her father and brother. In adolescence, under the influence of evangelical doctrine, she became fervently religious and even, in a moment of extreme piety, rejected fiction as suitable reading. Her position was perhaps uncomfortable for a family whose religious doctrines were generally easy-going, but not impossible to accept. Real difficulty came in 1842, when the reading and discussion of historical criticism of the Bible with a free-thinking circle in Coventry led her to reject its supernatural content. There was a painful estrangement from her father, finally settled by a compromise which maintained her intellectual integrity without sacrificing her family ties. She agreed to attend church with her father, and he allowed her thoughts to go their own way.

During the next twelve years George Eliot did intellectual work which contributed to the main currents of Victorian thought. In the Midlands and later London she completed translations of Strauss's *Life of Jesus* and Feuerbach's *Essence of Christianity* from the German, and began one of Spinoza's *Ethics* from the Latin. She also wrote for leading London journals, especially the liberal *Westminster Review*, which she also edited for two years. At the same time the need for a life of feeling was not dormant, a fact revealed not only in many sensitive and affectionate letters to friends, but also in the incomplete record we have of a love affair with another editor of the *Westminster Review*, John Chapman. Some years later, in 1854, came the action which was to scandalize her society, cast her out from her family, and open her career as a novelist. She eloped with George Henry Lewes, a married man, who could not divorce his wife because he had condoned her previous adultery. Lewes provided the combination of emotional security and intellectual stimulus she was always seeking. Mercurial, buoyant, and affectionate, he was a versatile talent who wrote books on acting, physiology, philosophy, and zoology, as well as two novels and a famous biography of the German poet Goethe. He provided a good counterbalance to her much more introspective nature.

With Lewes' encouragement, she began to write fiction. The first fruit, three stories about rural clergymen, appeared in parts in *Blackwood's Magazine*, 1857-58. She adopted the pseudonym, George Eliot, partly to avoid the prejudice against women writers, and partly, one suspects, to shield herself from direct criticism to which she was always hypersensitive. One year later her first novel, *Adam Bede*, appeared to great acclaim and popularity, and her reputation was established. Her identity was soon revealed, but she retained her pen-name for all her subsequent works : six novels, a verse-drama, one volume of poetry and one of essays. Her reputation remained high through her lifetime. She died in 1880, two years after Lewes, and six months after a second and orthodox marriage which finally won a communication from her brother Isaac, silent since learning of her union with Lewes, twenty-three years before.

Like all major writers George Eliot works within a tradition, consolidating and building on the work of others. She is perhaps most obviously traditional in the Victorian form of her novels, which like those of her contemporaries are written on a larger scale than most written today, with an abundance of characters, incidents, details, and events. With such a scale the Victorian novelist was able to give a comprehensive picture of a society, in the variety of its groups and in the interaction among them. He was also left with room to comment on and interpret the characters, actions and themes of his presentations. Such comment is perhaps the most distinguishing feature of Victorian fiction, and reaches one of its highest points of development in George Eliot's work, where the author's presence contributes to an extraordinary range of ironic, comic and pathetic effects. This convention of omniscient authorial comment has been criticized as disrupting 'fictional illusion' by reminding us of the outside world, but this now seems too naïve a view, a generalization based on examples which may indeed have been clumsy, obvious, or otherwise mismanaged. This book will provide several examples from which the reader may draw his own conclusions.

George Eliot not only works within a tradition in adopting the novel form of her contemporaries, but also in drawing on specific writers who inspire or affect her work. There is her contemporary, John Ruskin, the third volume of whose *Modern Painters* she reviewed in 1856, noting particularly his emphasis on 'realism—the doctrine that all truth and beauty are to be attained by a humble and faithful study of nature'—an emphasis which we also find in her fiction. There is the work of the classical Greek tragedians, which influenced her conception of the tragic form she was to adapt for the novel. And one may go back (as she does) to Cervantes' *Don Quixote* to see one source of a theme which she is to exploit in a particularly psychological manner, the problem of separating illusion from reality. But more significant influences are two writers, one romantic and one classical, whose major works were being completed only a few years before she was born. They are Wordsworth and Jane Austen.

Wordsworth leaves his mark especially on the early works, Jane Austen on the late. Like many of Wordsworth's poems the stories of *Scenes of Clerical Life* and the novels *Adam Bede* and *Silas Marner* deal with humble and rustic life, and if George Eliot's rustics are the less idealized and more realistic, her aim is his: to show the dignity and worth of an unsophisticated society and people. As well, many passages in the early works show a Wordsworthian quality of luminescence in their style, the quality of 'emotion recollected in tranquillity'. This is especially true of *The Mill on the Floss*, a 'novel of memory', concerned, like Wordsworth's *Prelude*, with the psychological development of a human being from childhood, the formative power of the past on the present. Jane Austen's influence shows especially in the satiric note brought to bear on the more genteel society of the later novels, especially *Middlemarch* and *Daniel Deronda*. Here we see her fools and egoists, as well as George Eliot's version of her wise and humane figures. At times there are remarkably direct echoes: we see the ancestor of Gwendolen in *Daniel Deronda* in Jane Austen's *Emma*, like her, witty, egotistical and manipulative, like her, too unpleasant to be totally charming and too charming to be totally unpleasant.

If Jane Austen seems to influence the late novels, and Wordsworth the early, there is one respect in which the influence of both is always present. It lies in George Eliot's moral ideas, which represent a fusion of the views of both authors. Of course, we should not interpret 'moral ideas' in any narrow sense, but rather in the sense of Matthew Arnold's phrase, the study of 'how to live'. For Wordsworth this meant the opposite of following an abstract code of human behaviour. Rather, the 'moral being' lay in the response of human being to human need, the extension of our fellow feeling. This too is George Eliot's view: the aim of her art is to 'enlarge our sympathies', and the demonstration of such enlargement is embodied in her novels, which always contain scenes which highlight the moving and restorative influence of one human being on another. But such a notion lacks a social dimension, which Jane Austen supplies. If we require sympathy to understand and live with our fellows, we also require judgement. Jane Austen sees the basis of that judgement in a moral order which will restrain, control, and reform the destructive impulses of the ego, and her emphasis is also George Eliot's. There are some differences in conception: Jane Austen tends to see the order in the established values of society, while George Eliot, less certain of those values, sees it more in general concepts of duty and self-sacrifice, but its function in both is the same: to implicitly and ironically comment on characters, and to provide the basis for their possible restoration.

George Eliot works within a tradition and adds to that tradition. Her works point to the future as well as the past. Some of these advances have been suggested: she extends the novel's range of subject matter in emphasizing ordinary lives and situations as suitable subjects for fiction, and indeed for tragic treatment. Original too is her emphasis on the work which occupies most of mankind much of the time. George Eliot shows her characters at work, or wondering about the meaning of their work, or wondering about the work they should do. And she presents some larger issues arising out of that showing: how society may make creative work possible or imposs- ible, or the role of that creative work in making a full human being. There are other issues raised of immediate relevance today, among them the social role of women (as with Dorothea in *Middlemarch*), the relation of educa- tion to individual and social need (as with Tom Tulliver in *The Mill on the Floss*) or the difficulty of maintaining a sense of human community in a growing and complex society (implicit or explicit in all the novels). And in terms of technical contribution we can point especially to the later novels, where passages rendering the inner lives of the characters are remarkably like the 'dramatized con- sciousness' of the novels of Henry James, and therefore one step away from the 'stream of consciousness' of the modern novels of Virginia Woolf or James Joyce. Similarly we can see another kind of emphasis on inner life—the inner life of memory—which, present in most of her fiction and especially in *The Mill on the Floss*, is developed from Wordsworth and is to leave its mark on the greatest modern novelist of memory, Marcel Proust. Or we can point to *Daniel Deronda*, with its use of flashback to bind together two parallel plots, its openness of beginning and ending, or its attempt in one of the plots to transform many of the conventions of the novel form. Like all major artists George Eliot leads us to new possibilities, for fiction and for life.

Scheme of extracts

This Profile emphasizes original and traditional sides to George Eliot's genius. The first two sections, on 'Milieu' and 'Approach to Character' illustrate especially the powers of sociological and psychological insight and analysis which are generally recognized as the distinctive features of her imagination. The second two sections, on 'Dialogue' and 'Narrative', illustrate especially more traditional (and somewhat neglected) novelistic strengths where we may see that imagination, literally, in action. Throughout, the analysis following the extracts will emphasize the artistic techniques which create the effects illustrated. In all sections the arrangement of extracts is chronological, so that there will be an incidental (though only incidental) outline of the novelist's development. I have given very full representation to the major novels most likely to be read by the student, especially to *Adam Bede*, *The Mill on the Floss*, *Middlemarch*, and *Daniel Deronda*, which may therefore be treated as individual profiles. There are no extracts from *Romola* or the early *Scenes of Clerical Life*. All references are to the definitive Cabinet Edition (Edinburgh, 1878-80).

Milieu

George Eliot's novels are set mainly in the rural community or village, or in the provincial town. There are exceptions in the historical novel *Romola*, set in sixteenth-century Florence, and *Daniel Deronda*, unusual in its variety of English and continental settings, but that is the pattern. She is not a novelist of the major urban centre, as were her contemporaries, Dickens and Thackeray.

To rural and provincial life she brings her novelist's version of the sociological imagination, so that we are constantly made aware of the economic and social forces which help determine individual lives. Her study of society is not, however, 'scientifically neutral', as that of a social scientist might be. It is rather informed by a moral imagination which is at once unpatronizing and unevasive, scrupulously rendering the strengths and limitations of any given society. Emphasis varies from novel to novel, but we may generally say that with the larger and more complex societies of the later novels there is both a greater emphasis on limitations, and a more critical tone in their presentation. The faults of the small centre, when stressed, are seen to be those of parochialism—narrow-mindedness and complacency—but those of the larger may include these and add some of its own. These are products of its complexity: increasing individual alienation and social impersonality. To be sure, some sense of community persists, but one feels that it fights a losing battle. It is significant that in the later novels we are frequently forced to think of milieu in terms of social class rather than society, for the characters themselves have lost contact with the total social life. Below we will examine in detail the milieux of individual novels and the means by which we are given a sense of their changing quality.

Adam Bede is a rural tragedy, showing the destructive impact on a stable farming community of the seduction of a milkmaid, Hetty Sorrel, by Arthur Donnithorne, son of the local squire. A major symbol of the vitality and stability of that community is the Hall Farm, leased from the squire by Mr and Mrs Poyser, Hetty's uncle and aunt. In a sense, too, the farm remains a symbol throughout George Eliot's fiction, for the duties and affections embodied in its way of life are never forgotten as values by which society is to be judged.

I

Plenty of life there! though this is the drowsiest time of the year, just before hay-harvest; and it is the drowsiest time of the day too, for it is close upon three by the sun, and it is half-past three by Mrs Poyser's handsome eight-day clock. But there is always a stronger sense of life when the sun is brilliant after rain; and now he is pouring down his beams, and making sparkles among the wet straw, and lighting up every patch of vivid green moss on the red tiles of the cow-shed, and turning even the muddy water that is hurrying along the channel to the drain into a mirror for the yellow-billed ducks, who are seizing the opportunity of getting a drink with as much body in it as possible. There is quite a concert of noises: the great bulldog, chained against the stables, is thrown into furious exasperation by the unwary approach of a cock too near the mouth of his kennel, and sends forth a thundering bark, which is answered by two fox-hounds shut up in the opposite cow-house; the old top-knotted hens, scratching with their chicks among the straw, set up a sympathetic croaking as the discomfited cock joins them; a sow with her brood, all very muddy as to the legs, and curled as to the tail, throws in some deep staccato notes; our friends the calves are bleating from the home croft; and, under all, a fine ear discerns the continuous hum of human voices.

For the great barn-doors are thrown wide open, and men are busy there mending the harness, under the superintendence of Mr Goby the 'whittaw', otherwise saddler, who entertains them with the latest Treddleston gossip. It is certainly rather an unfortunate day that Alick, the shepherd, has chosen for having the whittaws, since the morning turned out so wet; and Mrs Poyser has spoken her mind pretty strongly as to the dirt which the extra number of men's shoes brought into the house at dinnertime. Indeed, she has not yet recovered her equanimity on the subject, though it is now nearly three hours since dinner, and the house-floor is perfectly clean again; as clean as everything else in that wonderful house-place, where the only chance of collecting a few grains of dust would be to climb on the salt-coffer, and put your finger on the high mantel-shelf on which the glittering brass candle-sticks are enjoying their summer sinecure; for at this time of year, of course, every one goes to bed while it is yet light, or at least light enough to discern the outline of objects after you have bruised your shins against them. Surely nowhere else could an oak clock-case and an oak table have got to such a polish by the hand : genuine 'elbow polish', as Mrs Poyser called it, for she thanked God she never had any of your varnished rubbish in her house.

Adam Bede, ch. 6

The passage is unusual in George Eliot's fiction but typical of *Adam Bede* in that the presentation of milieu is unanalytic. The language is that of total acceptance, all warmth and no irony. The presentation might be called 'idyllic' were it not for the toughening effect of its realism, a realism which should not be seen, however, as cool or disillusioned rendering, but rather as a kind of circumstantiality, what George Eliot calls the 'faithful representing of commonplace things'. That kind of realism is never to be quite the same in her fiction, and is to disappear almost altogether in the later works. Here we see it in such details as the 'yellow-billed ducks' and the 'old top-knotted hens' of the barnyard, or the 'glittering brass candle-sticks' in the house. Such details are built up cumulatively, in a series of leisurely clauses, and both their abundance and the lazy manner of clausal procedure help to create our sense of the richness and stability of the farm and the way of life it represents. In the second section of the passage characters are introduced, notably Mrs Poyser, and the casual, almost anecdotal account of their activities has a similar effect. A sense of continuity through time is created as well by a variety of means, among them the reporting of customary farm activities as well as those at work on this particular occasion. Sometimes very commonplace stylistic details have functions too easily overlooked : one might consider, for example, the effect of the persistent choice of the definite over the indefinite article.

The rich, anecdotal quality of background rendering seen in *Adam Bede* is still present in George Eliot's next novel, *The Mill on the Floss*, but it is mixed with a new note, analytic and more critical. The following passage might be contrasted with the one above; its quality is not just that of something recollected in rich detail, but also of something understood by an intelligence which tries to see it in historical depth and assess it by historical comparison. St Ogg's is an old provincial town by the river Floss, and George Eliot has been talking about the floods which ravaged it in the past. Mrs Glegg is the aunt of the novel's heroine, Maggie Tulliver.

2

But the town knew worse troubles even than the floods —troubles of the civil wars, when it was a continual fighting-place where first Puritans thanked God for the blood of the Loyalists, and then Loyalists thanked God for the blood of the Puritans. Many honest citizens lost all their possessions for conscience' sake in those times and went forth beggared from their native town. Doubtless there are many houses standing now on which those honest citizens turned their backs in sorrow; quaint-gabled houses looking on the river, jammed between newer warehouses and penetrated by surprising passages which turn and turn at sharp angles till they lead you out on a muddy strand overflowed continually by the rushing tide. Everywhere the brick houses have a mellow look, and in Mrs Glegg's day there was no incongruous new-fashioned smartness, no plate-glass in shop windows, no fresh stuc-co-facing or other fallacious attempt to make fine old red St Ogg wear the air of a town that sprang up yesterday. The shop windows were small and unpretending, for the farmers' wives and daughters who came to do their shop-ping on market-days were not to be withdrawn from their regular, well-known shops, and the tradesmen had no wares intended for customers who would go on their way and be seen no more. Ah! Even Mrs Glegg's day seems far back in the past now, separated from us by changes that widen the years. War and the rumour of war had then died out from the minds of men, and if they were ever thought of by the farmers in drab greatcoats, who shook the grain out of their sample-bags and buzzed over it in the full market-place, it was as a state of things that belonged to a past golden age, when prices were high. Surely the time was gone forever when the broad river could bring up unwelcome ships; Russia was only the place where the linseed came from—the more the better —making grist for the great vertical millstones with their scythelike arms, roaring and grinding and carefully sweeping as if an informing soul were in them. The Catholics, bad harvests, and the mysterious fluctuations of trade were the three evils mankind had to fear; even the floods had not been great of late years. The mind of St Ogg's did not look extensively before or after. It inherited a long past without thinking of it and had no eyes for the spirits that walk the streets. Since the centuries when St Ogg with his boat and the Virgin Mother at the prow had been seen on the wide water, so many memories had been left behind and had gradually vanished like the receding hill-tops! And the present time was like the level plain where men lose their belief in volcanoes and earth-quakes, thinking tomorrow will be as yesterday and the giant forces that used to shake the earth are forever laid to sleep. The days were gone when people could be greatly wrought upon by their faith, still less change it; the Catholics were formidable because they would lay hold of government and property and burn men alive, not because any sane and honest parishioner of St Ogg's could be brought to believe in the Pope. One aged person remembered how a rude multitude had been swayed when John Wesley preached in the cattle-market, but for a long while it had not been expected of preachers that they should shake the souls of men. An occasional burst of fervour in Dissenting pulpits on the subject of infant baptism was the only symptom of a zeal unsuited to sober times when men had done with change. Protestantism sat at ease, unmindful of schisms, careless of proselytism; Dissent was an inheritance along with a superior pew and a business connection; and Churchmanship only wondered contemptuously at Dissent as a foolish habit that clung greatly to families in the grocery and chandlering lines, though not incompatible with prosperous wholesale dealing.

The Mill on the Floss, Bk. I, ch. 12

There are two main periods of time contrasted in this passage: the troubled past in which the town was subject to dangers from floods and civil and foreign war, and in which its citizens could be moved by issues of patriotism and faith, and the more stable present of self-satisfied business activity. The past is used to shed an ironic light on the present, whose comfortable self-sufficiency really derives from blindness to the larger forces that move nature and mankind, whose conservatism is seen not as an awareness of history, but as an attempt to escape from its processes. George Eliot is here dealing with what in other hands might have been an essay, but as a novelist her achievement is to make the abstract and concrete work hand in hand, so that the analysis of the town becomes inseparable from its imaginative recreation. So, for example, the general comment 'War and the rumour of war had then died out from the minds of men' is syntactically and logically linked with 'the farmers in drab greatcoats' and the detail of their activities, as well as with the echo of their speech in the final phrases of the sentence linking the golden age with high prices. Such echo of complacent local speech is common in the passage ('Russia was only the place where the linseed came from —the more the better'), falling somewhere between out- right quotation and outright parody, and illustrating dramatically the provincial quality of mind elsewhere analysed. The whole passage is a good example of the use of the omniscient author convention; note, however, the one more personal comment *within* that convention: 'Ah! Even Mrs Glegg's day seems far back in the past now,

separated from us by changes that widen with the years.'
The voice is that of the future, now seeing as history that
time when 'men had done with change', and ironically
judging it, but it is also a personal voice, not without a
sense of loss.

Maggie Tulliver, the novel's heroine, grows up near St
Ogg's, and the novel is in good part the record of the
conflict between her idealistic, yet ardent and romantic
temperament and the conventionality of the town. Both
her passion and idealism are seen in the final book of the
novel, where Maggie is drawn into a compromising situation with her cousin's fiancé, Stephen Guest, then chooses
not to marry him. In the following passage George Eliot
defines the community as she presents its reaction to
these events in the chapter titled 'St Ogg's Passes
Judgement'.

3

It was soon known throughout St Ogg's that Miss Tulliver was come back; she had not, then, eloped in order to
be married to Mr Stephen Guest; at all events, Mr
Stephen Guest had not married her, which came to the
same thing so far as her culpability was concerned. We
judge others according to results; how else, not knowing
the process by which results are arrived at? If Miss
Tulliver, after a few months of well-chosen travel, had
returned as Mrs Stephen Guest with a post-marital
trousseau and all the advantages possessed even by the
most unwelcome wife of an only son, public opinion,
which at St Ogg's, as elsewhere, always knew what to
think, would have judged in strict consistency with those
results. Public opinion in these cases is always of the
feminine gender—not the world, but the world's wife
—and she would have seen that two handsome young

people—the gentleman of quite the first family in St Ogg's—having found themselves in a false position, had been led into a course which, to say the least of it, was highly injudicious and productive of sad pain and disappointment, especially to that sweet young thing, Miss Deane. Mr Stephen Guest had certainly not behaved well, but then, young men were liable to those sudden infatuated attachments; and bad as it might seem in Mrs Stephen Guest to admit the faintest advances from her cousin's lover (indeed it *had* been said that she was actually engaged to young Wakem; old Wakem himself had mentioned it), still she was very young. 'And a deformed young man, you know! And young Guest so very fascinating; and they say he positively worships her (to be sure, that can't last!) and he ran away with her in the boat quite against her will—and what could she do? She couldn't come back then; no one would have spoken to her; and how very well that maize-coloured satinette becomes her complexion! It seems as if the folds in front were quite come in; several of her dresses are made so; they say he thinks nothing too handsome to buy for her. Poor Miss Deane! She is very pitiable; but then, there was no positive engagement; and the air at the coast will do her good. After all, if young Guest felt no more for her than *that*, it was better for her not to marry him. What a wonderful marriage for a girl like Miss Tulliver— quite romantic! Why, young Guest will put up for the borough at the next election. Nothing like commerce nowadays! That young Wakem nearly went out of his mind; he always *was* rather queer; but he's gone abroad again to be out of the way, quite the best thing for a deformed young man. Miss Unit declares she will never visit Mr and Mrs Stephen Guest. Such nonsense! Pretending to be better than other people. Society couldn't be carried on if we inquired into private conduct in that way, and Christianity tells us to think no evil; and my belief is that Miss Unit had no cards sent her.'

The Mill on the Floss, Bk. VII, ch. 2

Here the revelation of society comes not through analysis but through an ironic representation of the collective community voice, or at least its female section: the 'world's wife', a phrase which itself neatly captures the presumption of those who think of themselves as guardians of the world's morals. By giving all the women one voice in a current of indirect speech George Eliot also makes another point: these firm assertive voices by speaking in chorus reveal themselves to be unthinkingly timid and conformist. The passage reveals two conceptions of morality, that of the idealist, Maggie, who sees it in terms of attitudes of heart and self-sacrifice, and that of the 'respectable', who see it in terms of keeping up appearances. George Eliot is a comic as well as tragic writer, and here we see some of her ironic comedy at its best. Some of the comedy comes from the author's own remarks ('public opinion, which at St Ogg's, as elsewhere, always knew what to think'), but even more comes from the self-revelation of the speakers, whose lip service to feeling and morality is betrayed by shallowness of tone ('productive of sad pain and disappointment'), by phrases which let slip their real values ('young Guest will put up for the borough at the next election'), or by the rationalizations whose speciousness is transparent ('Society couldn't be carried on if we inquired into private conduct in that way').

With *Silas Marner* we return to a more genial though not uncritical presentation of milieu. The novel is set in the village of Raveloe at the time of the Napoleonic wars. In the following passage George Eliot uses the occasion of the introduction of Squire Cass, whose son Godfrey is the main figure in one of the novel's two actions, to develop a sense of the social structure of the village.

4

The greatest man in Raveloe was Squire Cass, who lived
in the large red house, with the handsome flight of
stone steps in front and the high stables behind it, nearly
opposite the church. He was only one among several
landed parishioners, but he alone was honoured with the
title of Squire; for though Mr Osgood's family was also
understood to be of timeless origin—the Raveloe imagination having never ventured back to that fearful blank
when there were no Osgoods—still, he merely owned the
farm he occupied; whereas Squire Cass had a tenant or
two, who complained of the game to him quite as if he
had been a lord.

It was still that glorious wartime which was felt to be a
peculiar favour of Providence towards the landed interest,
and the fall of prices had not yet come to carry the
race of small squires and yeomen down that road to ruin
for which extravagant habits and bad husbandry were
plentifully anointing their wheels. I am speaking now in
relation to Raveloe and the parishes that resembled it;
for our old fashioned country life had many different
aspects, as all life must have when it is spread over a
various surface, and breathed on variously by multi-
tudinous currents, from the winds of heaven to the
thoughts of men, which are forever moving and crossing
each other, with incalculable results. Raveloe lay low
among the bushy trees and the rutted lanes, aloof from
the currents of industrial energy and Puritan earnestness:
the rich ate and drank freely, and accepted gout and
apoplexy as things that ran mysteriously in respectable
families, and the poor thought that the rich were entirely
in the right of it to lead a jolly life; besides, their feasting
caused a multiplication of orts, which were the heirlooms
of the poor. Betty Jay scented the boiling of Squire Cass's
hams, but her longing was arrested by the unctuous liquor
in which they were boiled; and when the seasons brought

round the great merrymakings, they were regarded on all hands as a fine thing for the poor. For the Raveloe feasts were like the rounds of beef and the barrels of ale—they were on a large scale, and lasted a good while, especially in the winter time. When ladies had packed up their best gowns and top knots in band boxes, and had incurred the risk of fording streams on pillions with the precious burden in rainy or snowy weather, when there was no knowing how high the water would rise, it was not to be supposed that they looked forward to a brief pleasure. On this ground it was always contrived in the dark seasons, when there was little work to be done, and the hours were long, that several neighbours should keep open house in succession. When Squire Cass's standing dishes diminished in plenty and freshness, his guests had nothing to do but to walk a little higher up the village to Mr Osgood's, at the Orchards, and they found hams and chines uncut, pork pies with the scent of the fire in them, spun butter in all its freshness—everything, in fact, that appetites at leisure could desire, in perhaps greater perfection, though not in greater abundance, than at Squire Cass's.

Silas Marner, ch. 3

In *Silas Marner*, unlike *Adam Bede* or *The Mill on the Floss*, society is neither victim of nor agent in the main action. Yet the milieu is more than a mere context, for the village community with its weaknesses and strengths nourishes the individual, and the main story of the miser Silas is that of an individual's regaining of that nourishment. In this passage we get a balanced picture of community strengths and limitations, as the historian's sense of perspective gives us a notion of the complacencies, and the novelist's sympathy gives us a sense of the human life and warmth. The community is carefully placed in time and space: it is no idyllic place that never was, but rather one kind of parish existing in England at this time, 'aloof from the currents of industrial energy and Puritan earnestness', which affected the character of others. Its self-satisfaction is defined by authorial irony ('that fearful blank when there were no Osgoods', that 'glorious war-time'—for whom?), but the stress is on warm human life as well, developed in the picture of feasting and abundance built up in the final paragraph. The balance and fairness are characteristic of George Eliot: one aspect of her 'realism' is a refusal to sacrifice truth to moral simplification.

The most sustained confrontation between individual and community in George Eliot comes in *Middlemarch*, between Lydgate, a young doctor dedicated to furthering medical research, and the town of Middlemarch. Lydgate's up-to-date knowledge seems heretical to its established medical men, and his departures from time-honoured practices rouse a more general suspicion. Such credit as he does get seems hardly propitious, as the following passage indicates.

5

But in this doubtful stage of Lydgate's introduction he was helped by what we mortals rashly call good fortune. I suppose no doctor ever came newly to a place without making cures that surprised somebody—cures which may be called fortune's testimonials, and deserve as much credit as the written or printed kind. Various patients got well while Lydgate was attending them, some even of dangerous illnesses; and it was remarked that the new doctor with his new ways had at least the merit of bringing people back from the brink of death. The trash talked on such occasions was the more vexatious to Lydgate, because it gave precisely the sort of prestige which an incompetent and unscrupulous man would desire, and was sure to be imputed to him by the simmering dislike of the other medical men as an encouragement on his own part of ignorant puffing. But even his proud outspokenness was checked by the discernment that it was as useless to fight against the interpretations of ignorance as to whip the fog; and 'good fortune' insisted on using those interpretations.

Mrs Larcher having just become charitably concerned about alarming symptoms in her charwoman, when Dr Minchin called, asked him to see her then and there, and to give her a certificate for the Infirmary; whereupon after examination he wrote a statement of the case as one of tumour, and recommended the bearer Nancy Nash as an out-patient. Nancy, calling at home on her way to the Infirmary, allowed the staymaker and his wife, in whose attic she lodged, to read Dr Minchin's paper, and by this means became a subject of compassionate conversation in the neighbouring shops of Churchyard Lane as being afflicted with a tumour at first declared to be as large and hard as a duck's egg, but later in the day to be about the size of 'your fist'. Most hearers agreed that it would have to be cut out, but one had known of oil and another of 'squitchineal' as adequate to soften and reduce any lump in the body when taken enough of into the inside—the oil by gradually 'soopling', the squitchineal by eating away.

Meanwhile when Nancy presented herself at the Infirmary it happened to be one of Lydgate's days there. After questioning and examining her, Lydgate said to the house-surgeon in an undertone, 'It's not tumour: it's cramp.' He ordered her a blister and some steel mixture, and told her to go home and rest, giving her at the same time a note to Mrs Larcher, who, she said, was her best employer, to testify that she was in need of good food.

But by-and-by Nancy, in her attic, became portentously worse, the supposed tumour having indeed given way to the blister, but only wandered to another region with angrier pain. The staymaker's wife went to fetch Lydgate, and he continued for a fortnight to attend Nancy in her own home, until under his treatment she got quite well and went to work again. But the case continued to be described as one of tumour in Churchyard Lane and other streets—nay, by Mrs Larcher also; for when Lydgate's remarkable cure was mentioned to Dr Minchin, he naturally did not like to say, 'The case was not one of tumour, and I was mistaken in describing it as such,' but answered, 'Indeed! ah! I saw it was a surgical case, not of a fatal kind.' He had been inwardly annoyed, however, when he had asked at the Infirmary about the woman he had recommended two days before, to hear from the house-surgeon, a youngster who was not sorry to vex Minchin with impunity, exactly what had occurred: he privately pronounced that it was indecent in a general practitioner to contradict a physician's diagnosis in that open manner, and afterwards agreed with Wrench that Lydgate was disagreeably inattentive to etiquette. Lydgate did not make the affair a ground for valuing himself or (very particularly) despising Minchin, such rectification of misjudgements often happening among men of equal qualifications. But report took up this amazing case of tumour, not clearly distinguished from cancer, and considered the more awful for being of the wandering sort; till much prejudice against Lydgate's method as to drugs was overcome by the proof of his marvellous skill in the speedy restoration of Nancy Nash after she had been rolling and rolling in agonies from the presence of a tumour both hard and obstinate, but nevertheless compelled to yield.

Middlemarch, ch. 45

This passage resembles 'St Ogg's Passes Judgement' above, in that George Eliot is again suggesting, in compressed form, the irrational and self-flattering procedures of community judgement. Here, however, she is less displaying the conclusions drawn than the process by which they are reached, and for that reason chooses a different form: not the indirect collective speech of the ladies of St Ogg's, but narrative in which the growth of rumour can be traced, stage by stage. There remains, however, the

23

characteristic mimicry of community speech in all simple-mindedness: Lydgate has 'at least the merit of bringing people back from the brink of death', or 'the oil by gradually "soopling", the squitchineal by eating away'. The passage is built on a contrast between such lazy and ignorant thinking and the disciplined knowledge implicit in Lydgate's careful handling of cases, a contrast in which the other medical man, Dr Minchin, must be seen as leaning to the community side. But the contrast is not just between knowledge and ignorance, but also between power and the lack of it. The power here belongs to ignorance, not knowledge: as Lydgate finds, he can no more fight rumour than 'whip a fog'. The image is characteristic of many in the novel which define his condition in terms of frustration and impotence, and both image and passage suggest the tragedy to come.

In *Middlemarch* George Eliot gives us a picture of English provincial society at the time of the first reform bill of 1832. We have just seen one important section of that society. Another is the country gentry, of which the novel's heroine, Dorothea Brooke, is a member. But she is only uncomfortably so, her idealism often clashing with the settled values of her class, and, as she progresses morally, critically commenting on them. Here is one such comment from towards the novel's close. It is made through the reaction to Dorothea's engagement to Will Ladislaw, a young man of unfixed talents, who finds no real niche in Middlemarch society, and is clearly given some special status by the author for doing so. (Not all readers agree that he earns it.) There is reference throughout to a series of preceding events: Dorothea is now a widow, and her former husband Casaubon, intensely jealous of Ladislaw (his cousin), made provision in his will for Dorothea's disinheritance should she marry him. Any engagement, therefore, seems to confirm Casaubon's

24

imputations of Will's fortune-hunting and Dorothea's mis-
conduct. Here Dorothea's uncle, Mr Brooke, breaks the
news.

6

'Well, it's a very trying thing, you know,' said Mr Brooke.
'I'm glad you and the Rector are here; it's a family matter
—but you will help us all to bear it, Cadwallader. I've got
to break it to you, my dear.' Here Mr Brooke looked at
Celia—'You've no notion what it is, you know. And,
Chettam, it will annoy you uncommonly—but you see
you have not been able to hinder it, any more than I have.
There's something singular in things: they came round,
you know.'

'It must be about Dodo,' said Celia, who had been used
to think of her sister as the dangerous part of the family
machinery. She had seated herself on a low stool against
her husband's knee.

'For God's sake let us hear what it is!' said Sir James.

'Well, you know, Chettam, I couldn't help Casaubon's
will: it was a sort of will to make things worse.'

'Exactly,' said Sir James, hastily. 'But *what* is worse?'

'Dorothea is going to be married again, you know,' said
Mr Brooke, nodding towards Celia, who immediately
looked up at her husband with a frightened glance, and
put her hand on his knee.

Sir James was almost white with anger, but he did not
speak.

'Merciful heaven!' said Mrs Cadwallader. 'Not to young
Ladislaw?'

Mr Brooke nodded, saying, 'Yes; to Ladislaw,' and then
fell into a prudential silence.

'You see, Humphrey!' said Mrs Cadwallader, waving
her arm towards her husband. 'Another time you will
admit that I have some foresight; or rather you will contradict me and be just as blind as ever. *You* supposed that the

young gentleman was gone out of the country.'

'So he might be, and yet come back,' said the Rector, quietly.

'When did you learn this?' said Sir James, not liking to hear any one else speak, though finding it difficult to speak himself.

'Yesterday,' said Mr Brooke, meekly, 'I went to Lowick. Dorothea sent for me, you know. It had come about quite suddenly—neither of them had any idea two days ago— not any idea, you know. There's something singular in things. But Dorothea is quite determined—it is no use opposing. I put it strongly to her. I did my duty, Chettam. But she can act as she likes, you know.'

'It would have been better if I had called him out and shot him a year ago,' said Sir James, not from bloody-mindedness, but because he needed something strong to say.

'Really, James, that would have been very disagreeable,' said Celia.

'Be reasonable, Chettam. Look at the affair more quietly,' said Mr Cadwallader, sorry to see his good-natured friend so overmastered by anger.

'That is not so very easy for a man of any dignity— with any sense of right—when the affair happens to be in his own family,' said Sir James, still in his white indignation. 'It is perfectly scandalous. If Ladislaw had had a spark of honour he would have gone out of the country at once, and never shown his face in it again. However, I am not surprised. The day after Casaubon's funeral I said what ought to be done. But I was not listened to.'

'You wanted what was impossible, you know, Chettam,' said Mr Brooke. 'You wanted him shipped off. I told you Ladislaw was not to be done as we liked with: he had his ideas. He was a remarkable fellow—I always said he was a remarkable fellow.'

'Yes,' said Sir James, unable to repress a retort, 'it is rather a pity you formed that high opinion of him. We are indebted to that for him being lodged in this neighbourhood. We are indebted to that for seeing a woman like Dorothea degrading herself by marrying him.' Sir James made little stoppages between his clauses, the words not coming easily. 'A man so marked out by her husband's will, that delicacy ought to have forbidden her from seeing him again—who takes her out of her proper rank—into poverty—has the meanness to accept such a sacrifice—has always had an objectionable position—a bad origin—and, I *believe*, is a man of little principle and light character. That is my opinion,' Sir James ended emphatically, turning aside and crossing his leg.

'I pointed everything out to her,' said Mr Brooke, apologetically—'I mean the poverty, and abandoning her position. I said, "My dear, you don't know what it is to live on seven hundred a-year, and have no carriage, and that kind of thing, and go amongst people who don't know who you are." I put it strongly to her. But I advise you to talk to Dorothea herself. The fact is, she has a dislike to Casaubon's property. You will hear what she says, you know.'

'No—excuse me—I shall not,' said Sir James, with more coolness. 'I cannot bear to see her again; it is too painful. It hurts me too much that a woman like Dorothea should have done what is wrong.'

'Be just, Chettam,' said the easy, large-lipped Rector, who objected to all this unnecessary discomfort. 'Mrs Casaubon may be acting imprudently : she is giving up a fortune for the sake of a man, and we men have so poor an opinion of each other that we can hardly call a woman wise who does that. But I think you should not condemn it as a wrong action, in the strict sense of the word.'

'Yes, I do,' answered Sir James. 'I think that Dorothea commits a wrong action in marrying Ladislaw.'

Middlemarch, ch. 84

Middlemarch society at large tends to be conveyed through a panoramic authorial survey, but the milieu in which Dorothea moves is rendered much more through a refraction into individual voices, through dialogue. This refraction of course makes us conscious of the differences of personality seen in the reactions above: Mr Brooke drifting between appeasement and protest, Mrs Cadwallader, knowing in hindsight, the Rector Cadwallader, comfortably good-humoured, Sir James, outraged, and Celia, uncomprehending but loyal to an eccentric sister. Yet if there are differences in personality there are also the respectable class values of propriety and property held in common, and challenged by Dorothea's romantic engagement. No one suggests that the reality of her honourable behaviour in her previous marriage is more important than the appearance of dishonour, nor that wealth and position might be legitimately sacrificed to love rather than the reverse. George Eliot tends throughout to avoid a truly satiric note, which might be achieved easily, too easily, by making the characters social stereotypes. Sir James and Mr Brooke are the only ones close to satiric portraiture, but the satire of Mr Brooke is less of him as a class representative than as the liberal mind run amok, while that of Sir James is given human dimension by such means as Mr Cadwallader's reference to his 'good-natured friend', or by our awareness of the generous nature we have met elsewhere in the novel. Overall the passage is comic rather than satiric. It has been said that 'humour dissolves morality': one might consider whether or not the social issues raised here are partly dissolved by the humorous context.

Among the most brilliantly rendered scenes in George Eliot are those which take place among the English country aristocracy in *Daniel Deronda*: a higher and more influential class than the county gentry of *Middlemarch*. It is the main milieu of one of the novel's two actions, that involving the heroine, Gwendolen Harleth. Gwendolen is a newcomer to this society, and makes a striking impact,

which culminates in her marriage to the eminently eligible
Henleigh Grandcourt. But there is a bitter moral price to
her 'success': the marriage deprives Grandcourt's mistress
and their children of any hope of legitimacy, and Grandcourt himself is a refinedly brutal man, whose emotional
satisfactions come from a kind of psychological bullying.
Here we see a typical English social scene, with Gwendolen (here unmarried) the centre of attention, as usual.

7

Gwendolen's reception in the neighbourhood fulfilled
her uncle's expectations. From Brackenshaw Castle to the
Firs at Wancester, where Mr Quallon the banker kept a
generous house, she was welcomed with manifest admiration, and even those ladies who did not quite like her, felt a
comfort in having a new, striking girl to invite; for
hostesses who entertain much must make up their parties
as ministers make up their cabinets, on grounds other than
personal liking. Then, in order to have Gwendolen as a
guest, it was not necessary to ask any one who was disagreeable, for Mrs Davilow always made a quiet, picturesque figure as a chaperon, and Mr Gascoigne was everywhere in request for his own sake.

Among the houses where Gwendolen was not quite
liked and yet invited, was Quetcham Hall. One of her first
invitations was to a large dinner-party there, which made
a sort of general introduction for her to the society of the
neighbourhood; for in a select party of thirty and of well-
composed proportions as to age, few visitable families
could be entirely left out. No youthful figure there was
comparable to Gwendolen's as she passed through the long
suite of rooms adorned with light and flowers, and, visible
at first as a slim figure floating along in white drapery,
approached through one wide doorway after another into
fuller illumination and definiteness. She had never had that

sort of promenade before, and she felt exultingly that it befitted her: any one looking at her for the first time might have supposed that long galleries and lackeys had always been a matter of course in her life; while her cousin Anna, who was really more familiar with these things, felt almost as much embarrassed as a rabbit suddenly deposited in that well-lit space.

'Who is that with Gascoigne?' said the archdeacon, neglecting a discussion of military manœuvres on which, as a clergyman, he was naturally appealed to. And his son, on the other side of the room—a hopeful young scholar, who had already suggested some 'not less elegant than ingenious' emendations of Greek texts—said nearly at the same time, 'By George! who is that girl with the awfully well-set head and jolly figure?'

Daniel Deronda, ch. 5

The light satiric touch is typical of the rendering of many of the novel's scenes of 'society' and is a witty manifestation of a general criticism of its shallow commitments and superficial human relations. The first paragraph indicates such superficiality in a principle governing social life: not any deep or genuine feeling, but appearances. Gwendolen is 'new' and 'striking', and so invited for display, even if she is disliked. The image which follows puts such activity in satiric perspective: by implication, the hostesses think their party arrangements are as important as those of a government cabinet. The technique of juxtaposition of the serious with the trivial, each given equal rhetorical weight, is a mock-heroic technique not unlike that seen in Pope's *Rape of the Lock*, another satiric picture of 'society'. Satiric, too, are the clichés of the 'scholar' in the third paragraph: his learning does not seem to have rubbed his language into any freshness of perception. The serious theological matters discussed by the archdeacon speak for themselves.

It is not all satire, however. Mr Gascoigne, Gwendolen's uncle, a somewhat worldly rector, is genuinely and universally liked 'for his own sake', and the image of Anna, accompanying Gwendolen and feeling 'as much embarrassed as a rabbit' suddenly deposited in that 'well-lit space' is comic, with a touch of pathos, not satiric. One might consider the position of Gwendolen herself. Many readers of the *Rape of the Lock* have noticed how Belinda, the heroine, is admired by the author for her beauty and style as well as criticized for her superficial values. One might ask whether there is any evidence of a similar treatment of Gwendolen in this passage.

The critical comment on this important and influential section of English society is made not only satirically, but also by cultural contrast. The main contrast is with a milieu which the novelist, for obvious reasons, cannot present directly: the idea of a Jewish nation. The idea is embodied mainly in the prophetic vision of one character, Mordecai, and in the story of the hero, Deronda, an English gentleman who is to discover he is Jewish. There are, however, other and more indirect means of presentation. There are the scenes of domestic life, English and Jewish, where natural human relations and duties are in implicit contrast with the relatively artificial ones of sophisticated society. There is the liberating world of art. And there is the novel's geographical range, which suggests the insularity of this English culture by presenting foreign places (or characters) embodying alternative ways of life. Here is Deronda at Genoa, awaiting the first interview with his long-lost mother.

8

Day after day passed, and the very air of Italy seemed to carry the consciousness that war had been declared against Austria, and every day was a hurrying march of crowded Time towards the world-changing battle of Sadowa. Meanwhile, in Genoa, the noons were getting hotter, the converging outer roads getting deeper with white dust, the oleanders in the tubs along the wayside gardens looking more and more like fatigued holiday-makers, and the sweet evening changing her office—scattering abroad those whom the mid-day had sent under shelter, and sowing all paths with happy social sounds, little tinklings of mule-bells and whirrings of thrumbed strings, light footsteps and voices, if not leisurely, then with the hurry of pleasure in them; while the encircling heights, crowned with forts, skirted with fine dwellings and gardens, seemed also to come forth and gaze in fulness of beauty after their long siesta, till all strong colour melted in the stream of moonlight which made the streets a new spectacle with shadows, both still and moving, on cathedral steps and against the façades of massive palaces; and then slowly with the descending moon all sank in deep night and silence, and nothing shone but the port lights of the great Lanterna in the blackness below, and the glimmering stars in the blackness above. Deronda, in his suspense, watched this revolving of the days as he might have watched a wonderful clock where the striking of the hours was made solemn with antique figures advancing and retreating in monitory procession, while he still kept his ear open for another kind of signal which would have its solemnity too.

Daniel Deronda, ch. 50

This is a *tour de force*, the actual description of Genoa being conveyed in one superb sentence, whose easy progressive movement captures the constant features of the scene (the 'encircling lights', the 'forts', the 'fine dwellings and gardens') as well as the changing aspects and rhythms of work and leisure, light and shade, sun and moon. In the first sentence allusions are more historical than geographical, although they function similarly to enlarge awareness of human life apart from our own and therefore with lessons for our own.

The approach to character

The approach to character in George Eliot is first of all
that of most major realistic novelists. She creates a variety
of characters which is the image of society, and shows a
variety of individual response which is an image of
human complexity. But her approach may be more closely
defined. She is also a psychological novelist, who gives a
profound sense of the inner life which determines outward actions. And she is one of a special kind. Her
emphasis on the inner life comes most frequently (though
not invariably) when that inner life has moral implications, usually in its reflection of the self-deception of the
character, and often in the potential of that self-deception
for harm to others. She shows evasion of the issues in
fantasy or rationalization, or confrontation of them in
moral triumph. She is a psychologist especially of the
moral life. That moral life should not be seen, however,
in simple terms, but rather as a complex process which
may evoke our admiration or criticism, pity or terror.
Nearly all the main characters are shown as either growing out of or becoming further encased in what George
Eliot calls the 'moral stupidity' of egoism. Some characters
—the most destructive—are shown as permanently
imprisoned within this 'moral stupidity', while others are
shown to have escaped it entirely. These latter tend to

34

minister to and aid others who occupy positions somewhere between the extremes.

To portray the inner life of her characters George Eliot
uses a characteristic analytic technique, one which
distinguishes her from those novelists who suggest psychological issues mainly through the dramatic presentation
of a character's speech or actions. George Eliot always
uses such means, but adds to them a large element of
explanation. She shows us her characters' minds in action,
infusing with that demonstration her own interpretive
comment. The following passages will attempt to illustrate
the variety of effects achieved.

Adam Bede, a young carpenter, is the hero of the novel
of that name. There is some idealization in the presentation of Adam, but it is qualified in at least two ways. At
several points the author underlines a moral failing in
Adam's severity of judgement, his want of sympathetic
imagination. He is also given a realistic capacity for self-
deception, seen in the following passage. Adam, in love
with Hetty, is walking home from Arthur's birthday-feast,
disturbed by her alarm when her locket drops during a
dance, revealing two intertwined locks of hair.

9

Suddenly, when he was far on through the Chase, he
stopped, startled by a flash of reviving hope. After all, he
might be a fool, making a great misery out of a trifle.
Hetty, fond of finery as she was, might have bought the
thing herself. It looked too expensive for that—it looked
like the things on white satin in the great jeweller's shop at
Rosseter. But Adam had very imperfect notions of the
value of such things, and he thought it could certainly not
cost more than a guinea. Perhaps Hetty had had as much
as that in Christmas boxes, and there was no knowing

but she might have been childish enough to spend it in that way; she was such a young thing, and she couldn't help loving finery! But then, why had she been so frightened about it at first, and changed colour so, and afterwards pretended not to care? Oh, that was because she was ashamed of his seeing that she had such a smart thing—she was conscious that it was wrong for her to spend her money on it, and she knew that Adam disapproved of finery. It was a proof she cared about what he liked and disliked. She must have thought from his silence and gravity afterwards that he was very much displeased with her, that he was inclined to be harsh and severe towards her foibles. And as he walked on more quietly, chewing the cud of this new hope, his only uneasiness was that he had behaved in a way which might chill Hetty's feeling towards him. For this last view of the matter *must* be the true one. How could Hetty have an accepted lover, quite unknown to him? She was never away from her uncle's house for more than a day; she could have no acquaintances that did not come there, and no intimacies unknown to her uncle and aunt. It would be folly to believe that the locket was given to her by a lover. The little ring of dark hair he felt sure was her own; he could form no guess about the light hair under it, for he had not seen it very distinctly. It might be a bit of her father's or mother's, who had died when she was a child, and she would naturally put a bit of her own along with it.

And so Adam went to bed comforted, having woven for himself an ingenious web of probabilities—the surest screen a wise man can place between himself and the truth. His last waking thoughts melted into a dream that he was with Hetty again at the Hall Farm, and that he was asking her to forgive him for being so cold and silent.

And while he was dreaming this, Arthur was leading Hetty to the dance, and saying to her in low hurried tones, 'I shall be in the wood the day after tomorrow at seven; come as early as you can.'

Adam Bede, ch. 26

Here the self-deception takes a form not uncommon in George Eliot: that of rationalization. The structure of the passage is therefore that of debate, in which we move back and forth from argument to counter-argument. But the debate is bogus, for Adam's unconscious has predetermined the outcome in favour of his comforting illusions. Indeed, that such argument needs to take place at all should give him pause, though he dare not, in his fool's paradise, see that implication, just as he does not see the obvious implication of the obvious evidence. The first sentence of the second last paragraph is one of the few which are in the author's direct speech rather than Adam's indirect speech: one might ask if it is necessary or superfluous.

The Mill on the Floss is a semi-autobiographical novel presenting the development of its heroine, Maggie Tulliver, from childhood on. Central to this development is the relation between Maggie and her brother Tom. In the following passage we see first Maggie and then Tom in early adolescence, in their reaction to the disastrous failure of their father's quixotic lawsuit against a neighbour, a failure which breaks his health and reduces him to a tenancy on the land he formerly owned.

10

Maggie's sense of loneliness and utter privation of joy had deepened with the brightness of advancing spring. All the favourite outdoor nooks about home, which seemed to have done their part with her parents in nurturing and cherishing her, were now mixed up with the home-sadness and gathered no smile from the sunshine. Every affection, every delight the poor child had had was like an aching nerve to her. There was no music for her any more—no piano, no harmonized voices, no delicious stringed instruments with their passionate cries of imprisoned spirits sending a strange vibration through her frame. And of all her school-life there was nothing left her now but her little collection of school-books, which she turned over with a sickening sense that she knew them all and they were all barren of comfort. Even at school she had often wished for books with *more* in them; everything she learned there seemed like the ends of long threads that snapped immediately. And now—without the indirect charm of school-emulation—Télémaque was mere bran; so were the hard, dry questions on Christian doctrine; there was no flavour in them, no strength. Sometimes Maggie thought she could have been contented with absorbing fancies; if she could have had all Scott's novels and all Byron's poems, then perhaps she might have found happiness enough to dull her sensibility to her actual daily life. And yet . . . they were hardly what she wanted. She could make dream-worlds of her own but no dream-world would satisfy her now. She wanted some explanation of this hard, real life : the unhappy-looking father, seated at the dull breakfast-table; the childish, bewildered mother; the little sordid tasks that filled the hours, or the more oppressive emptiness of weary, joyless leisure; the need of some tender demonstrative love; the cruel sense that Tom didn't mind what she thought or felt, and that they were no longer playfellows together; the privation of all pleasant things that had come to *her* more than to others— she wanted some key that would enable her to understand, and in understanding endure, the heavy weight that had fallen on her young heart.

The Mill on the Floss, Bk. IV, ch. 3

Maggie's is the more complex of the two reactions. It begins in disenchantment, conveying in such pictures as that of the 'dull breakfast table' or the 'childish bewildered mother', her sense of a hard, unromantic reality. In this respect it resembles passages in the other novels marking stages in the development of the central characters. But in recognizing this similarity we should not overlook equally important differences. The passage is as much about depression as disenchantment, and the source of the depression is not the answer to questions about the nature of reality, but the lack of answers to questions about how to deal with it. Maggie has turned, without success, to a variety of resources which now seem themselves illusory: her school books, the romances of Scott and Byron, the world of imagination. All have inadequately dealt with a real world which is itself inadequate. There are perhaps two central phrases which suggest both the problem now and problems to come: the one at the close, describing her search for a 'key', and an earlier one describing her sense of absence in terms of absent music. The suggestion is that the key which Maggie seeks may well be, like the music, vaguely emotional, and therefore again illusory, a substitute for what the passage makes clear is really missing: love and understanding, particularly from Tom, who 'didn't mind what she thought and felt'.

Tom Tulliver has a different reaction to the family troubles. In order to save enough money to pay the family debts, he has gone to work for his uncle Deane.

II

But now Tom's strong will bound together his integrity, his pride, his family regrets, and his personal ambition, and made them one force, concentrating his efforts and surmounting discouragements. His uncle Deane, who watched him closely, soon began to conceive hopes of him and to be rather proud that he had brought into the employment of the firm a nephew who appeared to be made of such good commercial stuff. The real kindness of placing him in the warehouse first was soon evident to Tom, in the hints his uncle began to throw out that after

39

a time he might perhaps be trusted to travel at certain seasons and buy in for the firm various vulgar commodities with which I need not shock refined ears in this place; and it was doubtless with a view to this result that Mr Deane, when he expected to take his wine alone, would tell Tom to step in and sit with him an hour and would pass that hour in much lecturing and catechizing concerning articles of export and import with an occasional excursus of more indirect utility on the relative advantages to the merchants of St Ogg's of having goods brought in their own and in foreign bottoms—a subject on which Mr Deane, as a ship-owner, naturally threw off a few sparks when he got warmed with talk and wine. Already, in the second year, Tom's salary was raised; but all, except the price of his dinner and clothes, went home into the tin box; and he shunned comradeship lest it should lead him into expenses in spite of himself. Not that Tom was moulded on the spooney type of the industrious apprentice; he had a very strong appetite for pleasure, would have liked to be a tamer of horses and to make a distinguished figure in all neighbouring eyes, dispensing treats and benefits to others with well-judged liberality and being pronounced one of the finest young fellows of those parts; nay, he determined to achieve these things sooner or later, but his practical shrewdness told him that the means to such achievements could only lie for him in present abstinence and self-denial; there were certain milestones to be passed, and one of the first was the payment of his father's debts. Having made up his mind on that point, he strode along without swerving, contracting some rather saturnine sternness, as a young man is likely to do who has a premature call upon him for self-reliance. Tom felt intensely that common cause with his father which springs from family pride, and was bent on being irreproachable as a son; but his growing experience caused him to pass much silent criticism on the rashness and imprudence of his father's past conduct; their dispositions were not in sympathy, and Tom's face showed little radiance during his few home-hours. Maggie had an awe of him against which she struggled as something unfair to her consciousness of wider thoughts and deeper motives, but it was of no use to struggle. A character at unity with itself—that performs what it intends, subdues every counteracting impulse, and has no visions beyond the distinctly possible—is strong by its very negations.

The Mill on the Floss, Bk. V, ch. 2

The definition of a character's reactions is the definition of character. Tom's reactions are directed outward, towards the overcoming of obstacles in the real world, while Maggie turns inward, to overcome obstacles largely definable in terms of her emotional and imaginative life. An earlier paragraph (not quoted) suggests that the difference is to some extent sexual, but it is even more importantly one of temperament. Tom is of his mother's family, the Dodsons, while Maggie is of the more romantic Tullivers. The different reactions thus suggest a potentially tragic incompatibility between brother and sister and hint at the course of future action. Here both strengths and limitations of Dodson attitudes are stressed: Tom is in touch with reality, but the contact is unimaginative. He does not, like Maggie, have any sense of alternative values or ways of life, nor does he extend to others—here, his father—the tolerance and understanding which Maggie extends to him. It is all summed up in the final sentence, which underlines the narrowness which creates the strength.

Middlemarch has four main actions, of which three may be seen as love stories. The opening book of the novel, 'Miss Brooke', deals almost exclusively with one of these, that of the courtship of Dorothea Brooke by a middle-aged, pendantic clergyman and scholar, Mr Casaubon, and contains some of the liveliest humorous and satirical writing of the novel. In Dorothea we have another variant on egoism, not the obviously self-seeking kind, but that which dramatizes the self in a set of idealistic and selfless postures and attitudes. The satire is never harsh, for Dorothea's egoism is the less culpable both for its selfless form and for its innocence: she lacks experience and (a point made emphatically) any kind of education except the useless one given to 'ladies' of the time. She is not a hypocrite but simply too young and ignorant to know herself and the world. Most of these points emerge in the following passage. Celia is Dorothea's more orthodox sister.

12

And how should Dorothea not marry?—a girl so handsome and with such prospects? Nothing could hinder it but her love of extremes, and her insistence on regulating life according to notions which might cause a wary man to hesitate before he made her an offer, or even might lead her at last to refuse all offers. A young lady of some birth and fortune, who knelt suddenly down on a brick floor by the side of a sick labourer and prayed fervidly as if she thought herself living in the time of the Apostles —who had strange whims of fasting like a Papist, and of sitting up at night to read old theological books! Such a wife might awaken you some fine morning with a new scheme for the application of her income which would interfere with political economy and the keeping of saddle-horses: a man would naturally think twice before he risked himself in such fellowship. Women were expected to have weak opinions; but the great safeguard of society and of domestic life was, that opinions were not acted on. Sane people did what their neighbours did, so that if any lunatics were at large, one might know and avoid them.

The rural opinion about the new young ladies, even among the cottagers, was generally in favour of Celia, as being so amiable and innocent-looking, while Miss Brooke's large eyes seemed, like her religion, too unusual and striking. Poor Dorothea! compared with her, the innocent-looking Celia was knowing and worldly-wise; so much subtler is a human mind than the outside tissues which make a sort of blazonry or clock-face for it.

Yet those who approached Dorothea, though prejudiced against her by this alarming hearsay, found that she had a charm unaccountably reconcilable with it. Most men thought her bewitching when she was on horseback. She loved the fresh air and the various aspects of the country, and when her eyes and cheeks glowed with mingled pleasure she looked very little like a devotee. Riding was an indulgence which she allowed herself in spite of conscientious qualms; she felt that she enjoyed it in a pagan sensuous way, and always looked forward to renouncing it.

She was open, ardent, and not in the least self-admiring; indeed, it was pretty to see how her imagination adorned her sister Celia with attractions altogether superior to her own, and if any gentleman appeared to come to the Grange from some other motive than that of seeing Mr Brooke, she concluded that he must be in love with Celia: Sir James Chettam, for example, whom she constantly considered from Celia's point of view, inwardly debating whether it would be good for Celia to accept him. That he should be regarded as a suitor to herself would have seemed to her a ridiculous irrelevance. Dorothea, with all her eagerness to know the truths of life, retained very childlike ideas about marriage. She felt sure that she would have accepted the judicious Hooker, if she had been born in time to save him from that wretched mistake he made in matrimony; or John Milton when his blindness had come on; or any of the other great men whose odd habits it would have been glorious piety to endure; but an amiable handsome baronet, who said 'Exactly' to her remarks even when she expressed uncertainty,—how could he affect her as a lover? The really delightful marriage must be that where your husband was a sort of father, and could teach you even Hebrew, if you wished it.

Middlemarch, ch. 1

The light satiric strokes cut two ways in the passage: we have both the comic spectacle of a young lady dropping to her knees to pray with alarming unpredictability, and its viewing by the conventional male member of society who fears for the implications for 'political economy and the keeping of saddle-horses': presumably indistinguishable in the mind of a gentleman. George Eliot's powers of mimicry give the life here and throughout: the authorial 'telling' adopts variously the vocabulary and attitudes of community, suitor, and Dorothea, as well as its own definitive voice. So we hear how 'so much subtler is a human mind than the outside tissues which make a sort of blazonry or clock-face for it': the author's admonition on us not to accept any superficial view of a human essence, and then, later, in a summary of attitudes which could almost be Dorothea's slip of tongue, how she enjoyed riding, she 'always looked forward to renouncing it'.

There is a subtle transition in the final paragraph, as we move almost imperceptibly from general description to the action, or rather to the specific situation from which action is to come. This inconspicuous management of transitions is one of the distinguishing features of George Eliot's late style. Here the unnamed suitors of the previous paragraph take on a name, Sir James Chettam, and Dorothea, so marriageable, takes on an attitude to marriage. It is a highly unrealistic one, first manifest in her comic misreading of Sir James' attentions to her, and then in the exposition of her fantasies on the subject. These have several implications. The choice of Hooker or Milton as ideal partners is grandiose, and a reflection of self-importance. But it is also idealistic, both in the sense of involving self-sacrifice, however glibly conceived, and in the sense of representing an aim more noble than that immediately achievable in the 'amiable handsome baronet' whose limitations, if not intentions, Dorothea sees perceptively enough. Above all the fantasy is innocent: a marriage, even to Milton, would not be simply one where 'a husband was a sort of father, and could teach you even Hebrew'.

The idea of a gentleman is a recurrent theme in George Eliot's fiction as it is in English fiction up to the turn of the century. Most writers pay at least as much attention to characters who fail to live up to such gentlemanly ideals as courtesy, considerateness, and moderation, as to those who succeed, and George Eliot is no exception. She frequently portrays young men whose education has given them nothing of practical social value and themselves an exalted sense of their own importance. This sense of presumptuousness built into social role merges, in varying degrees, with a more general sense of the presumptuous and dangerously beguiling self-importance of youth, but with Fred Vincy in *Middlemarch* (as with Stephen Guest in *The Mill on the Floss*) the social emphasis is particularly strong. Fred is ultimately to wed Mary Garth in the novel, but he first must prove himself, and here we see him off to the worst possible start, twice borrowing money on his 'expectations' of an inheritance to pay debts for horses and gambling, and using the signature of Mary's father, Caleb, as surety for the loans.

13

On both occasions Fred had felt confident that he should meet the bill himself, having ample funds at disposal in his own hopefulness. You will hardly demand that his confidence should have a basis in external facts; such confidence, we know, is something less coarse and materialistic: it is a comfortable disposition leading us to expect that the wisdom of providence or the folly of our friends, the mysteries of luck or the still greater mystery of our high individual value in the universe, will bring about agreeable issues, such as are consistent with our good taste in costume, and our general preference for the best style of thing. Fred felt sure that he should have a present from his uncle, that he should have a run of luck, that by dint of 'swapping' he should gradually metamorphose a horse worth forty pounds into a horse that would fetch a hundred at any moment—'judgement' being always equivalent to an unspecified sum in hard cash. And in any case, even supposing negations which only a morbid distrust could imagine, Fred had always (at that time) his father's pocket as a last resource, so that his assets of hopefulness had a sort of gorgeous superfluity about them. Of what might be the capacity of his father's pocket. Fred had only a vague notion : was not trade elastic? And would not the deficiencies of one year be made up for by the surplus of another? The Vincys lived in an easy profuse way, not with any new ostentation, but according to the family habits and traditions, so that the children had no standard of economy, and the elder ones retained some of their infantine notion that their father might pay for anything if he would. Mr Vincy himself had expensive Middlemarch habits—spent money on coursing, on his cellar, and on dinner-giving, while mamma had those running accounts with tradespeople, which give a cheerful sense of getting everything one wants without any question of payment. But it was in the nature of fathers, Fred knew, to bully one about expenses : there was always a little storm over his extravagance if he had to disclose a debt, and Fred disliked bad weather within doors. He was too filial to be disrespectful to his father, and he bore the thunder with the certainty that it was transient; but in the meantime it was disagreeable to see his mother cry, and also to be obliged to look sulky instead of having fun; for Fred was so good-tempered that if he looked glum under scolding, it was chiefly for propriety's sake. The easier course, plainly, was to renew the bill with a friend's signature. Why not? With the superfluous securities of hope at his command, there was no reason why he should not have increased other people's liabilities to any extent, but for the fact that men whose names were good for anything were usually pessimists, indisposed to believe that the universal order of things would necessarily be agreeable to an agreeable young gentleman.

Middlemarch, ch. 23

Here is none of the lightness of touch with which Dorothea was satirized, because there is nothing to warrant it. Fred is smug: Dorothea is not; Fred uses others; Dorothea does not. The satiric technique is to use Fred's vocabulary, complacent in its very slanginess, as a means of ironically revealing his lazy, comfortable assumptions. There is only slight distortion, either through inflation (facts are 'coarse and materialistic', or the 'mysteries of luck' work for us), or through crisp deflation ('the still greater mystery of our high individual value in the universe'). The technique perhaps reaches a high point in the vague notion of trade being 'elastic', a word which indeed captures Fred's basic assumption about his father's pocket. Towards the last half of the passage we have some idea given of the Vincy home life, and more important, an emphasis on Fred's attitudes in human relations: he 'disliked bad weather', it was 'disagreeable to see his mother cry'. Here, as in money-matters and speech, he takes the easy way out: his strongest awareness is of any threat to his own comfort, rather than of his threat to that of others. Egocentricity so systematic is 'providential': Fred's unconscious assumption is that the Divine intention and his own are indistinguishable, and George Eliot defines it, characteristically, with a metaphor from book-keeping.

In viewing the collision course of the fantasies of her central characters and the reality which operates on laws indifferent to them, George Eliot's voice, either explicitly in authorial comment or implicitly in narrative tone, achieves a wide range of tragic, comic and pathetic effects.

It is perhaps the pathos which brings us closest to character, and certainly the pathos which is most distinctively the note of George Eliot. Her comic effects have been compared to those of Jane Austen, and her tragic effects to those of Aeschylus and Hardy, but for the pathetic it is other writers who have be compared to her. The reason lies, I think, in the absence of sentimentality : there is deep sympathy for ordinary, low-pitched human suffering, but it is controlled by moral judgement and critical intelligence. We are not only made aware of the sufferer, but also of the choices and circumstances which led to his situation. Such awareness reaches a high point in George Eliot's art in the portrayal of Mr Casaubon in *Middlemarch*. Here he is shortly after his marriage to Dorothea.

14

One morning, some weeks after her arrival at Lowick, Dorothea—but why always Dorothea? Was her point of view the only possible one with regard to this marriage? I protest against all our interest, all our effort at understanding being given to the young skins that look blooming in spite of trouble; for these too will get faded, and will know the older and more eating griefs which we are helping to neglect. In spite of the blinking eyes and white moles objectionable to Celia, and the want of muscular curve which was morally painful to Sir James, Mr Casaubon had an intense consciousness within him, and was spiritually a-hungered like the rest of us. He had done nothing exceptional in marrying—nothing but what society sanctions, and considers an occasion for wreaths and bouquets. It had occurred to him that he must not any longer defer his intention of matrimony, and he had reflected that in taking a wife, a man of good position should expect and carefully choose a blooming young lady— the younger the better, because more educable and sub-

48

missive—of a rank equal to his own, of religious principles, virtuous disposition, and good understanding. On such a young lady he would make handsome settlements, and he would neglect no arrangement for her happiness: in return, he should receive family pleasures and leave behind him that copy of himself which seemed so urgently required of a man—to the sonneteers of the sixteenth century. Times had altered since then, and no sonneteer had insisted on Mr Casaubon's leaving a copy of himself; moreover, he had not yet succeeded in issuing copies of his mythological key; but he had always intended to acquit himself by marriage, and the sense that he was fast leaving the years behind him, that the world was getting dimmer and that he felt lonely, was a reason to him for losing no more time in overtaking domestic delights before they too were left behind by the years.

And when he had seen Dorothea he believed that he had found even more than he demanded: she might really be such a helpmate to him as would enable him to dispense with a hired secretary, an aid which Mr Casaubon had never yet employed and had a suspicious dread of. (Mr Casaubon was nervously conscious that he was expected to manifest a powerful mind.) Providence, in its kindness, had supplied him with the wife he needed. A wife, a modest young lady, with the purely appreciative, unambitious abilities of her sex, is sure to think her husband's mind powerful. Whether Providence had taken equal care of Miss Brooke in presenting her with Mr Casaubon was an idea which could hardly occur to him. Society never made the preposterous demand that a man should think as much about his own qualifications for making a charming girl happy as he thinks of hers for making himself happy. As if a man could choose not only his wife but his wife's husband! Or as if he were bound to provide charms for his posterity in his own person!—When Dorothea accepted him with effusion, that was only natural; and Mr Casaubon believed that his happiness was going to begin.

49

He had not had much foretaste of happiness in his previous life. To know intense joy without a strong bodily frame, one must have an enthusiastic soul. Mr Casaubon had never had a strong bodily frame, and his soul was sensitive without being enthusiastic: it was too languid to thrill out of self-consciousness into passionate delight; it went on fluttering in the swampy ground where it was hatched, thinking of its wings and never flying. His experience was of that pitiable kind which shrinks from pity, and fears most of all that it should be known: it was that proud narrow sensitiveness which has not mass enough to spare for transformation into sympathy, and quivers thread-like in small currents of self-preoccupation or at best of an egoistic scrupulosity. And Mr Casaubon had many scruples: he was capable of a severe self-restraint; he was resolute in being a man of honour according to the code; he would be unimpeachable by any recognized opinion. In conduct these ends had been attained; but the difficulty of making his Key to all Mythologies unimpeachable weighed like lead upon his mind; and the pamphlets—or 'Parerga' as he called them—by which he tested his public and deposited small monumental records of his march, were far from having been seen in all their significance. He suspected the Archdeacon of not having read them; he was in painful doubt as to what was really thought of them by the leading minds of Brasenose, and bitterly convinced that his old acquaintance Carp had been the writer of that depreciatory recension which was kept locked in a small drawer of Mr Casaubon's desk, and also in a dark closet of his verbal memory. These were heavy impressions to struggle against, and brought that melancholy embitterment which is the consequence of all excessive claim: even his religious faith wavered with his wavering trust in his own authorship, and the consolations of the Christian hope in immortality seemed to lean on the immortality of the still unwritten Key to all Mythologies. For my part I am very sorry for him. It is an uneasy lot at best, to be what we call highly taught and yet not to enjoy: to be present at this great spectacle of life and never to be liberated from a small hungry shivering self—never to be fully possessed by the glory we behold, never to have our consciousness rapturously transformed into the vividness of a thought, the ardour of a passion, the energy of an action, but always to be scholarly and uninspired, ambitious and timid, scrupulous and dim-sighted.

Middlemarch, ch. 29

The passage, we notice, breaks off from a discussion of Dorothea in an apparently spontaneous manner, as though the thought had just occurred to the author that she was yielding to the immoral temptation to consider a young, attractive human being as more important than an aging, unattractive one. Whether this is a record of how it was really written or whether it was planned that way is irrelevant to the effect: a point is made dramatically, in author's mid-thought, which we might have missed if she had simply presented Casaubon's consciousness. We start out complacently, and are then jolted into an awareness of the universe we had overlooked, and the author is implicated with us.

It is worth noticing that ironic and comic effects are not absent: 'no sonneteer had insisted on Mr Casaubon's leaving a copy of himself; moreover, he had not yet succeeded in issuing copies of his mythological key', but they assume a melancholy wryness in the context of a larger condition: 'the world was getting dimmer and . . . he felt lonely'. The larger condition emphasized in this line is the human one of being subject to aging and mortality but there are also limitations specifically those of Casaubon. These are defined in prose as rich in imagery as in analytic discrimination: the 'psychological notation' which is so definitive a feature of the late style. We not only hear that Casaubon's soul 'was too languid to thrill out of self-consciousness into passionate delight', but also how 'it went on fluttering in the swampy ground in which it was hatched, thinking of its wings and never flying'. The main feature of Casaubon's personality so defined is a caution which he might see as prudence but which we see as fear. His reluctance to publish—or marry—is too obviously defensive of a grandiose, secret self-concept implicit in the title of his work, the 'Key to All Mythologies'. Dorothea only seems a suitable partner because she is viewed as an adjunct to the 'Key': a substitute for a 'hired secretary', a 'modest young lady, with the purely appreciative, unambitious qualities of her sex'. (George Eliot does not miss the opportunity to score society's role in forming this conventional view of woman.) In the final sentences George Eliot speaks to us directly, as in the beginning, to make a personal appeal for Casaubon, and to underline his pathos by emphasizing his loss: never to be 'liberated' from egoism and fantasy into the richness of life.

Daniel Deronda shows more awareness of abnormal mental states and abnormal personalities than any other of George Eliot's novels. The heroine, Gwendolen, is subject to hysterical attacks, and a sexual coldness is more than hinted at, while Grandcourt, her suitor and later her husband, is an English gentleman whose conduct has sadistic overtones.

15

Grandcourt's thoughts this evening were like the circlets one sees in a dark pool continually dying out and continually started again by some impulse from below the surface. The deeper central impulse came from the image of Gwendolen; but the thoughts it stirred would be imperfectly illustrated by a reference to the amatory poets of all ages.

It was characteristic that he got none of his satisfaction from the belief that Gwendolen was in love with him; and that love had overcome the jealous resentment which had made her run away from him. On the contrary, he believed that this girl was rather exceptional in the fact that, in spite of his assiduous attention to her, she was not in love with him; and it seemed to him very likely that if it had not been for the sudden poverty which had come over her family, she would not have accepted him. From the very first there had been an exasperating fascination in the tricksiness with which she had—not met his advances, but —wheeled away from them. She had been brought to accept him in spite of everything—brought to kneel down like a horse under training for the arena, though she might have an objection to it all the while. On the whole, Grand-court got more pleasure out of this notion than he could have done out of winning a girl of whom he was sure that she had a strong inclination for him personally. And yet this pleasure in mastering reluctance flourished along with the habitual persuasion that no woman whom he favoured could be quite indifferent to his personal in-fluence; and it seemed to him not unlikely that by-and-by Gwendolen might be more enamoured of him than he of her. In any case she would have to submit; and he enjoyed thinking of her as his future wife, whose pride and spirit were suited to command every one but himself. He had no taste for a woman who was all tenderness to him, full of petitioning solicitude and willing obedience. He meant to be master of a woman who would have liked to master him, and who perhaps would have been capable of master-ing another man.

Daniel Deronda, ch. 28

The passage presents Grandcourt's interest in Gwendolen in terms which are scarcely reassuring. The image of the first line defines his mind in a manner which strikes at our most primitive human fears: of darkness and water in the 'dark pool', and of unknown and invisible life within them in the 'some impulse' which agitates it. We can scarcely feel more comfortable as the 'impulse' is almost immediately specified as the image of Gwendolen, for now the picture is of a human being lost in the darkness, drowned. Following such a sentence the phrase 'imperfectly illustrated by a reference to the amatory poets of all ages' seems a rather defensive understatement, the stylistic equivalent of the nervous laugh. Grandcourt's desire is made clear enough : it is for dominance and even more for the gratifications of achieving it, gratifications defined with more than one kind of appropriateness by the imagery from horse-taming. The central insight he has of Gwendolen's character—into her disdain and self-sufficiency—has a quality something like that of the half-truth. Grandcourt does not see what we see : the brutal irony of Gwendolen meeting her match in a distorted version of her own egoism.

The enlarged awareness of reality which marks the moral development of most of the main characters and helps to make that development a major action in the novels is always given vivid and dramatic emphasis, but with the exception of *Silas Marner*, the novels do not give us any one particular crisis as the major turning point. George Eliot is not a novelist of the overnight conversion. The crises should rather be regarded as stages in a process of gradual change. They usually reach a culmination towards the novels' close : in Adam's adjustment to the facts of the betrayal by Arthur and Hetty, or in Dorothea's conquest of her jealousy in her effort to save Lydgate's marriage. Here is perhaps the best stroke of all : Gwendolen, learning from and leaning on Deronda, has fallen in love with him, while all the while he has been moving towards another destiny as a Jew. Here Gwendolen (her husband now dead) learns of Deronda's decision to leave England and work with his people.

There was a long silence between them. The world seemed getting larger round poor Gwendolen, and she more solitary and helpless in the midst. The thought that he might come back after going to the East, sank before the bewildering vision of these wide-stretching purposes in which she felt herself reduced to a mere speck. There comes a terrible moment to many souls when the great movements of the world, the larger destinies, which have lain aloof in newspapers and other neglected reading, enter like an earthquake into their own lives—when the slow urgency of growing generations turns into the tread of an invading army or the dire clash of civil war, and grey fathers know nothing to seek for but the corpses of their blooming sons, and girls forget all vanity to make lint and bandages which may serve for the shattered limbs of their betrothed husbands. Then it is as if the Invisible Power that has been the object of lip-worship and lip-resignation became visible, according to the imagery of the Hebrew poet, making the flames of his chariot and riding on the wings of the wind, till the mountains smoke and the plains shudder under the rolling, fiery visitation. Often the good cause seems to lie prostrate under the thunder of unrelenting force, the martyrs live reviled, they die, and no angel is seen holding forth the crown and the palm branch. Then it is that the submission of the soul to the Highest is tested, and even in the eyes of frivolity life looks out from the scene of human struggle with the awful face of duty, and a religion shows itself which is something else than a private consolation.

That was the sort of crisis which was at this moment beginning in Gwendolen's small life: she was for the first time feeling the pressure of a vast mysterious movement, for the first time being dislodged from her supremacy in her own world, and getting a sense that her horizon was but a dipping onward of an existence with which her own was revolving. All the troubles of her wifehood and widowhood had still left her with the implicit impression which had accompanied her from childhood, that whatever surrounded her was somehow specially for her, and it was because of this that no personal jealousy had been roused in her in relation to Deronda: she could not spontaneously think of him as rightfully belonging to others more than to her. But here had come a shock which went deeper than personal jealousy—something spiritual and vaguely tremendous that thrust her away, and yet quelled all anger into self-humiliation.

Daniel Deronda, ch. 69

This is a splendidly orchestrated passage, in which both the imagery and (especially in the first paragraph) the movement of the clauses define the enlargement of Gwendolen's consciousness. The first paragraph shows a kind of explosion of awareness in which the self is left chastened and reduced. The larger forces of history embodied in Deronda's choice are defined by images of war, apocalypse and martyrdom, and long rolling clausal structures reduce Gwendolen's place in the paragraph both figuratively and quantitatively. The second paragraph turns from this awareness of the forces lying outside self to a more quiet emphasis on the new, disturbed inner life. It follows from the religious image which concluded the first paragraph, embodying the psychology if not using the language of religious conversion. Gwendolen feels 'dislodged' from her egoism, her horizon is 'but a dipping onward of an existence with which her own was revolving', her feelings make 'personal jealousy' irrelevant. She is losing, in a word, her egocentric sense of uniqueness, 'that whatever surrounded her was specially for her'.

Dialogue

Dialogue in the novel functions something like close-up in cinema. It brings out detail emphatically, momentarily neglecting the wider movement of event, of which it may be the culmination. It necessarily throws a stress on character, since words spoken reflect their speakers, however subtly and obliquely. It plays an important part in George Eliot's fiction, placing in dramatic context those characters whose inner lives we have elsewhere experienced, and showing us some of the implications of those inner lives for social living. It provides a balance to more analytic elements in her fiction, and reflects an important and often underrated side to her creative powers. She is a superb ventriloquist. She presents us with an extraordinary range of characters' voices, capturing both the idiom of social class and of the individual member of that class. We range from the village and peasant voices of *Adam Bede* to those of the international set in *Daniel Deronda*, from the faltering simplicity of Hetty Sorrel in the first of these novels to the energetic and allusive idiom of Klesmer in the latter. Only occasionally does a character's voice approximate too closely to that of the author, so that we lose a sense of his individual presence. When this happens it is usually in circumstances similar to those described below.

One recurrent and not always successful kind of dialogue in the fiction is that of the moral exchange. It nearly
always takes place between characters who have achieved
knowledge of self and reality and those who have not, in
a relationship which has been variously described as
priestly, psychotherapeutic or tutorial. Such adjectives
perhaps apply particularly to the less artistically successful relationships, like that between Daniel and Gwendolen
Harleth in *Daniel Deronda*. There are others, like that
between Dolly Winthrop and Silas in *Silas Marner*, or
between Farebrother and Fred Vincy in *Middlemarch*, that
proceed so easily and naturally that terms suggesting soul-
fulness or didacticism simply do not come to mind. Here
is an exchange which seems to me to come between the
extremes. Arthur Donnithorne is visiting the Reverend
Irwine, intending to discuss his growing involvement with
Hetty Sorrel, and here objects to a point raised by Irwine.

17

'But I think it is hardly an argument against a man's
general strength of character, that he should be apt to be
mastered by love. A fine constitution doesn't insure one
against smallpox or any other of those inevitable diseases.
A man may be very firm in other matters, and yet be under
a sort of witchery from a woman.'

'Yes; but there's this difference between love and smallpox, or bewitchment either—that if you detect the disease
at an early stage and try change of air, there is every
chance of complete escape, without any further development of symptoms. And there are certain alternative doses
which a man may administer to himself by keeping unpleasant consequences before his mind : this gives you a
sort of smoked glass through which you may look at the

resplendent fair one and discern her true outline; though I'm afraid, by the by, the smoked glass is apt to be missing just at the moment it is most wanted. I daresay, now, even a man fortified with a knowledge of the classics might be lured into an imprudent marriage, in spite of the warning given him by the chorus in the Prometheus.'

The smile that flitted across Arthur's face was a faint one, and instead of following Mr Irwine's playful lead, he said, quite seriously—'Yes, that's the worst of it. It's a desperately vexatious thing, that after all one's reflections and quiet determinations, we should be ruled by moods that one can't calculate on beforehand. I don't think a man ought to be blamed so much if he is betrayed into doing things in that way, in spite of his resolutions.'

'Ah, but the moods lie in his nature, my boy, just as much as his reflections did, and more. A man can never do anything at variance with his own nature. He carries within him the germ of his most exceptional action; and if we wise people make eminent fools of ourselves on any particular occasion, we must endure the legitimate con-clusion that we carry a few grains of folly to our ounce of wisdom.'

'Well, but one may be betrayed into doing things by a combination of circumstances, which one might never have done otherwise.'

'Why, yes, a man can't very well steal a bank-note, unless the bank-note lies within convenient reach; but he won't make us think him an honest man because he begins to howl at the bank-note for falling in his way.'

'But surely you don't think a man who struggles against a temptation into which he falls at last, as bad as the man who never struggles at all?'

'No, certainly; I pity him in proportion to his struggles, for they foreshadow the inward suffering which is the worst form of Nemesis. Consequences are unpitying. Our deeds carry their terrible consequences, quite apart from any fluctuations that went before—consequences that are hardly ever confined to ourselves. And it is best to fix our minds on that certainty, instead of considering what may be the elements of excuse for us. But I never knew you so inclined for moral discussion, Arthur? Is it some danger of your own that you are considering in this philosophical, general way?'

Adam Bede, ch. 16

The dialogue in this passage is a little too pat. Arthur always asks the right question or makes the right comment to allow Irwine to both rebut him and develop another point in the exposition on free will, responsibility and consequences, an exposition which represents George Eliot's own doctrines at this time. We have here a dramatization of doctrine, but it is one in which touches of the essay form—both in wording and in systematic rational structure—have not been entirely ironed out. Yet it is a dramatization. There is the genial informality framing the patches of exposition which keep the Reverend Irwine distinctly the speaker, and, more significantly, there is Arthur's characteristic self-deception at work. He keeps raising objections because he does not want to face the truth, and talks in general terms for the same reason. His characteristic defence is to camouflage his desires by a demonstration of his good nature and good intentions, a defence at work here as elsewhere. He goes on to ignore the advice as he has ignored the issues.

The next passage, also from *Adam Bede*, functions in a manner directly opposite to the one just quoted. If the first passage was almost too nakedly an exposition of doctrine underlying the novel, this passage can only with some strain be related to its themes at all. This is not necessarily a defect, for all fiction contains elements which cannot be tidily packaged in a critical scheme, and often these are the elements which most engage the reader. Victorian novels in particular are rich in material which has little function beyond demonstrating its own nature and creating that sense of abundance which Victorian critics called 'life'. In this scene, which takes place after the major action is over, the name of Dinah Morris, being courted by Adam, has come up in conversation, inspiring the misogynist village schoolmaster, Bartle Massey, and, in turn, Mrs Poyser.

18

'What!' said Bartle, with an air of disgust. 'Was there a woman concerned? Then I give you up, Adam.'

'But it's a woman you'n spoke well on, Bartle,' said Mr Poyser. 'Come, now, you canna draw back; you said once as women wouldna ha' been a bad invention if they'd all been like Dinah.'

'I meant her voice, man—I meant her voice, that was all,' said Bartle. 'I can bear to hear her speak without wanting to put wool in my ears. As for other things, I daresay she's like the rest o' the women—thinks two and two 'ull come to make five, if she cries and bothers enough about it.'

'Ay, ay!' said Mrs Poyser; 'one 'ud think, an' hear some folks talk, as the men war 'cute enough to count the corns in a bag o' wheat wi' only smelling at it. They can see through a barn-door, *they* can. Perhaps that's the reason they can see so little o' this side on't.'

Martin Poyser shook with delighted laughter, and winked at Adam, as much as to say the schoolmaster was in for it now.

'Ah!' said Bartle, sneeringly, 'the women are quick enough—they're quick enough. They know the rights of a story before they hear it, and can tell a man what his thoughts are before he knows 'em himself.'

'Like enough,' said Mrs Poyser; 'for the men are mostly so slow, their thoughts overrun 'em, an' they can only catch 'em by the tail. I can count a stocking-top while a man's getting's tongue ready; an' when he outs wi' his speech at last, there's little broth to be made on't. It's your dead chicks take the longest hatchin'. Howiver, I'm not denyin' the women are foolish: God Almighty made 'em to match the men.'

'Match!' said Bartle; 'ay, as vinegar matches one's teeth. If a man says a word, his wife'll match it with a contradiction; if he's a mind for hot meat, his wife 'll match it with cold bacon; if he laughs, she'll match him with whimpering. She's such a match as the horse-fly is to th' horse: she's got the right venom to sting him with—the right venom to sting him with.'

'Yes,' said Mrs Poyser, 'I know what the men like—a poor soft, as 'ud simper at 'em like the pictur o' the sun, whether they did right or wrong, an' say thank you for a kick, an' pretend she didna know which end she stood uppermost, till her husband told her. That's what a man wants in a wife, mostly; he wants to make sure o' one fool as 'ull tell him he's wise. But there's some men can do wi'out that—they think so much o' themselves a'ready; an' that's how it is there's old bachelors.'

'Come, Craig,' said Mr Poyser, jocosely, 'you mun get married pretty quick, else you'll be set down for an old bachelor; an' you see what the women 'ull think on you.'

'Well,' said Mr Craig, willing to conciliate Mrs Poyser, and setting a high value on his own compliments, 'I like a cleverish woman—a woman o' sperrit—a managing woman.'

'You're out there, Craig,' said Bartle, dryly; 'you're out there. You judge o' your garden-stuff on a better plan than that: you pick the things for what they can excel in—for what they can excel in. You don't value your peas for their roots, or your carrots for their flowers. Now, that's the way you should choose women: their cleverness 'll never come to much—never come to much; but they make excellent simpletons, ripe and strong-flavoured.'

'What dost say to that?' said Mr Poyser, throwing himself back and looking merrily at his wife.

'Say!' answered Mrs Poyser, with dangerous fire kindling in her eye; 'why, I say as some folks' tongues are like the clocks as run on strikin', not to tell you the time o' the day, but because there's summat wrong i' their own inside' . . .

Adam Bede, ch. 53

This is 'free' dialogue, displayed for its own sake, for the delight in the speech. It illuminates character, but not subtly, for that would throw attention away from the comic jousting and undermine the broad confrontation between Mrs Poyser's tidal energy and Bartle Massey's breakwater stubbornness. Some of the humour derives from this conflict of character, and some from the traditional echo of the war of the sexes which it evokes, but at least equally humour comes from the wit of the words themselves. It is as though Mrs Poyser and Bartle were trying less to win the argument than to outdo each other in rich folk inventiveness. Particularly remarkable is the pace and economy with which this is done: each statement of rebuttal works up, by a process of associative links, to an unexpected, yet in retrospect perfectly prepared climax: 'and that's how it is there's old bachelors'. Just as the dialogue as a whole has little beyond local significance, so the imagery it contains. The comparison of Mrs Poyser to a vegetable, or of Bartle to a clock in the two last paragraphs, evokes no echo from the outside context. Such images are common to all the fiction, but in the later we notice much more the recurrent images which tend to form a systematic pattern with symbolic overtones.

The Mill on the Floss is unusual in George Eliot's fiction in the dominant role played by secondary characters. In tracing the destinies of Tom and Maggie from childhood on this novel also necessarily focuses on their family, with its uncles and aunts as well as more immediate

parents. Most of the novel—up until the final book, where
the children are more autonomous young adults—can be
read as the story of that family, and particularly as the
story of the destiny of Mr Tulliver, whose choleric, impul-
sive nature is brought into confrontation with that of
the more respectable Dodsons. Here the Dodson aunts
(there are four sisters, including Mrs Tulliver), with their
husbands, are visiting the Tullivers, and have been told
of Mr Tulliver's plans to have Tom tutored by a clergyman.
Part of the meaning of the scene comes from a preceding
event to which reference is made: the loan of £500 from
Mrs Clegg to Mr Tulliver. The mourning referred to ('wi'
gowns craped alike') is for Mrs Sutton, a friend but 'no
kin'.

19

'Well, if I may be allowed to speak, and it's seldom as
I am,' said Mrs Glegg with a tone of bitter meaning, 'I
should like to know what good is to come to the boy by
bringin' him up above his fortin.'

'Why,' said Mr Tulliver, not looking at Mrs Glegg, but
at the male part of his audience, 'you see, I've made
up my mind not to bring Tom up to my own business.
I've had my thoughts about it all along, and I made up
my mind by what I saw with Garnett and *his* son. I mean
to put him to some business as he can go into without
capital, and I want to give him an eddication as he'll be
even wi' the lawyers and folks, and put me up to a notion
now an' then.'

Mrs Glegg emitted a long sort of guttural sound with
closed lips that smiled in mingled pity and scorn.

'It 'ud be a fine deal better for some people,' she said
after that introductory note, 'if they'd let the lawyers
alone.'

'Is he at the head of a grammar school, then, this

clergyman—such as that at Market Bewley?' said Mr
Deane.

'No—nothing o' that,' said Mr Tulliver. 'He won't take
more than two or three pupils—and so he'll have the more
time to attend to 'em, you know.'

'Ah, and get his eddication done the sooner; they can't
learn much at a time when there's so many of 'em,' said
uncle Pullet, feeling that he was getting quite an insight
into this difficult matter.

'But he'll want the more pay, I doubt,' said Mr Glegg.

'Aye, aye, a cool hundred a year—that's all,' said Mr
Tulliver with some pride at his own spirited course. 'But
then, you know, it's an investment; Tom's eddication 'ull
be so much capital to him.'

'Aye, there's something in that,' said Mr Glegg. 'Well,
well, neighbour Tulliver, you may be right, you may be
right:

> When land is gone and money's spent,
> Then learning is most excellent.

I remember seeing those two lines wrote on a window
at Buxton. But us that have got no learning had better
keep our money, eh, neighbour Pullet?' Mr Glegg rubbed
his knees and looked very pleasant.

'Mr Glegg, I wonder *at* you,' said his wife. 'It's very
unbecoming in a man o' your age and belongings.'

'What's unbecoming, Mrs G.?' said Mr Glegg, winking
pleasantly at the company. 'My new blue coat as I've got
on?'

'I pity your weakness, Mr Glegg. I say it's unbecoming
to be making a joke when you see your own kin going
headlongs to ruin.'

'If you mean me by that,' said Mr Tulliver, considerably
nettled, 'you needn't trouble yourself to fret about me. I
can manage my own affairs without troubling other folks.'

'Bless me,' said Mr Deane, judiciously introducing a
new idea, 'why, now I come to think of it, somebody
said Wakem was going to send *his* son—the deformed

lad—to a clergyman, didn't they, Susan?' (appealing to his wife).

'I can give no account of it, I'm sure,' said Mrs Deane, closing her lips very tightly again. Mrs Deane was not a woman to take part in a scene where missiles were flying.

'Well,' said Mr Tulliver, speaking all the more cheerfully, that Mrs Glegg might see he didn't mind her, 'if Wakem thinks o' sending his son to a clergyman, depend on it I shall make no mistake i' sending Tom to one. Wakem's as big a scoundrel as Old Harry ever made, but he knows the length of every man's foot he's got to deal with. Aye, aye, tell me who's Wakem's butcher, and I'll tell you where to get your meat.'

'But Lawyer Wakem's son's got a hump-back,' said Mrs Pullet, who felt as if the whole business had a funereal aspect; 'it's more nat'ral to send *him* to a clergyman.'

'Yes,' said Mr Glegg, interpreting Mrs Pullet's observation with erroneous plausibility, 'you must consider that, neighbour Tulliver; Wakem's son isn't likely to follow any business. Wakem 'ull make a gentleman of him, poor fellow.'

'Mr Glegg,' said Mrs G. in a tone which implied that her indignation would fizz and ooze a little, though she was determined to keep it corked up, 'you'd far better hold your tongue. Mr Tulliver doesn't want to know your opinion nor mine neither. There's folks in the world as know better than everybody else.'

'Why, I should think that's you, if we're to trust your own tale,' said Mr Tulliver, beginning to boil up again.

'Oh, *I* say nothing,' said Mrs Glegg sarcastically. 'My advice has never been asked, and I don't give it.'

'It'll be the first time, then,' said Mr Tulliver. 'It's the only thing you're over-ready at giving.'

'I've been over-ready at lending, then, if I haven't been over-ready at giving,' said Mrs Glegg. 'There's folk I've lent money to, as perhaps I shall repent o' lending money to kin.'

'Come, come, come,' said Mr Glegg soothingly. But Mr Tulliver was not to be hindered of his retort.

'You've got a bond for it, I reckon,' he said; 'and you've had your five per cent, kin or no kin.'

'Sister,' said Mrs Tulliver pleadingly, 'drink your wine, and let me give you some almonds and raisins.'

'Bessy, I'm sorry for you,' said Mrs Glegg, very much with the feeling of a cur that seizes the opportunity of diverting his bark towards the man who carries no stick. 'It's poor work, talking o' almonds and raisins.'

'Lors, sister Glegg, don't be so quarrelsome,' said Mrs Pullet, beginning to cry a little. 'You may be struck with a fit, getting so red in the face after dinner, and we are but just out o' mourning, all of us—and all wi' gowns craped alike and just put by—it's very bad among sisters.'

'I should think it *is* bad,' said Mrs Glegg. 'Things are come to a fine pass when one sister invites the other to her house o' purpose to quarrel with her and abuse her.'

'Softly, softly, Jane—be reasonable—be reasonable,' said Mr Glegg.

But while he was speaking, Mr Tulliver, who had by no means said enough to satisfy his anger, burst out again.

'Who wants to quarrel with you?' he said. 'It's you as can't let people alone, but must be gnawing at 'em forever. *I* should never want to quarrel with any woman if she kept her place.'

'My place, indeed!' said Mrs Glegg, getting rather more shrill. 'There's your betters, Mr Tulliver, as are dead and in their grave, treated me with a different sort o' respect to what you do—though I've got a husband as'll sit by and see me abused by them as 'ud never ha' had the chance if there hadn't been them in our family as married worse than they might ha' done.'

'If you talk o' that,' said Mr Tulliver, 'my family's as good as yours—and better, for it hasn't got a damned ill-tempered woman in it.'

The Mill on the Floss, Bk. I, ch. 7

There are two versions of pride in conflict in this passage, each trying to impose his views on the audience. Mr Tulliver, more imaginative (and unrealistic) wants Tom to be a 'gentleman', fit to hold his own in a world which Mr Tulliver tends to have seen in conspiratorial terms of the educated perpetually foxing the less educated, while Mrs Glegg's is the more orthodox pride in family name and custom: why should Tom be extravagantly educated above his station, and why indeed should one desire any other station than that represented by Dodsons? It is for Mrs Glegg to use the respectable means of aggression in such an encounter: the 'tone of bitter meaning', the attitude of outraged decency, the 'guttural sound with closed lips that smiled with mingled pity and scorn', the address to the third party as though Mr Tulliver were not there or there but beyond redemption. Against these he has no defence but sarcasms culminating in an explosion of rage: he is, typically, too stubborn and too honest to really win a battle. The oblique style baffles and enrages the direct. We might notice, too, how speech reveals the other characters: in Mr Glegg's coarse, good-humoured management of himself and his wife, in Mr Deane's diplomacy, in Mrs Tulliver's helpless resignation, and in Mrs Pullet's characteristically gloomy remarks.

Perhaps the finest sections of George Eliot's *Felix Holt* deal with the relationship between Mrs Transome, a county lady, and her son, Harold. One should know, in reading the following passage, that Harold has just returned to England after a fifteen-year absence in Turkey, that, unknown to himself, his nominal father, and the community, he is an illegitimate child, and that his mother has for years fixed all her starved love and hopes on him. She has here been showing him her choice for his rooms.

As she turned round again she said, 'I suppose you have been used to great luxury; these rooms look miserable to you, but you can soon make any alteration you like.'

'O, I must have a private sitting-room fitted up for my-self down-stairs. And the rest are bedrooms, I suppose,' he went on, opening a side-door. 'Ah, I can sleep here a night or two. But there's a bedroom down-stairs, with an ante-room, I remember, that would do for my man Dominic and the little boy. I should like to have that.'

'Your father has slept there for years. He will be like a distracted insect, and never know where to go, if you alter the track he has to walk in.'

'That's a pity. I hate going up-stairs.'

'There is the steward's room: it is not used, and might be turned into a bedroom. I can't offer you my room, for I sleep up-stairs.' (Mrs Transome's tongue could be a whip upon occasion, but the lash had not fallen on a sensitive spot.)

'No; I'm determined not to sleep up-stairs. We'll see about the steward's room to-morrow, and I daresay I shall find a closet of some sort for Dominic. It's a nuisance he had to stay behind, for I shall have nobody to cook for me. Ah, there's the old river I used to fish in. I often thought, when I was at Smyrna, that I would buy a park with a river through it as much like the Lapp as possible. Gad, what fine oaks there are opposite! Some of them must come down, though.'

'I've held every tree sacred on the demesne, as I told you, Harold. I trusted to your getting the estate some time, and releasing it; and I determined to keep it worth releas-ing. A park without fine timber is no better than a beauty without teeth and hair.'

'Bravo, mother!' said Harold, putting his hand on her shoulder. 'Ah, you've had to worry yourself about things that don't properly belong to a woman—my father being

69

weakly. We'll set all that right. You shall have nothing to do now but to be grandmamma on satin cushions.'

'You must excuse me from the satin cushions. That is a part of the old woman's duty I am not prepared for. I am used to be chief bailiff, and to sit in the saddle two or three hours every day. There are two farms on our hands besides the Home Farm.'

'Phew-ew! Jermyn manages the estate badly, then. That will not last under *my* reign,' said Harold, turning on his heel and feeling in his pockets for the keys of his portmanteaus, which had been brought up.

Felix Holt, ch. 1

This is dialogue but not communication. Harold has no sense of his mother as a person, and only hears the bare sense of her words, whose emotional charge of pride and love bounces back painfully on herself. In a bitter irony—for her son's love of dominance is inherited from her—he simply denies her human autonomy, rearranging her plans, ignoring her sarcasm, dismissing her arguments, and patronizing her work. Harold is not indecorous, and is even, in a condescending way, tactful; George Eliot shows how superficial politeness is not the same as genuine sensitivity. He is a relatively good-natured example of a type to be explored in Rosamond and Grandcourt in the later fiction : the egoist of virtually total self-complacency, whose defences are second-nature and impenetrable.

Dialogue may reveal the deeper springs of personality not only in situations of conflict or psychological tension but also in more normal and apparently casual conversation. The record of a character's speech is also the record of the habitual perceptions of the world which determine it, in their strengths and limitations, depths and shallows. Sometimes this revelation may be very indirect and subtle, for language conceals as well as reveals, something which writers have long dramatized and Freud explained. This is particularly true of 'normal' conversation. where people do not 'let themselves go' as directly and from such deep sources as in a quarrel. *Middlemarch*, of all George Eliot's fiction, is notable for the number of such normal, quiet scenes and situations: here is one involving Mary Garth and Rosamond Vincy. Mary is tending her dying uncle, Peter Featherstone, at Stone Court, and Rosamond is visiting, ostensibly from casual motives, but really because she has learned that the fascinating young Doctor Lydgate has been tending the sick man. Miss Morgan is Rosamond's governess.

21

When she and Rosamond happened both to be reflected in the glass, she said laughingly—

'What a brown patch I am by the side of you, Rosy! You are the most unbecoming companion.'

'Oh no! No one thinks of your appearance, you are so sensible and useful, Mary. Beauty is of very little consequence in reality,' said Rosamond, turning her head towards Mary, but with eyes swerving towards the new view of her neck in the glass.

'You mean *my* beauty,' said Mary, rather sardonically.

Rosamond thought, 'Poor Mary, she takes the kindest things ill.' Aloud she said, 'What have you been doing lately?'

'I? Oh, minding the house—pouring out syrup—pretending to be amiable and contented—learning to have a bad opinion of everybody.'

'It is a wretched life for you.'

'No,' said Mary, curtly, with a little toss of her head. 'I think my life is pleasanter than your Miss Morgan's.'

'Yes; but Miss Morgan is so uninteresting, and not young.'

'She is interesting to herself, I suppose; and I am not at

all sure that everything gets easier as one gets older.'

'No,' said Rosamond, reflectively; 'one wonders what such people do, without any prospect. To be sure, there is religion as a support. But,' she added, dimpling, 'it is very different with you, Mary. You may have an offer.'

'Has any one told you he means to make me one?'

'Of course not. I mean, there is a gentleman who may fall in love with you, seeing you almost every day.'

A certain change in Mary's face was chiefly determined by the resolve not to show any change.

'Does that always make people fall in love?' she answered, carelessly; 'it seems to me quite as often a reason for detesting each other.'

'Not when they are interesting and agreeable. I hear that Mr Lydgate is both.'

'Oh, Mr Lydgate!' said Mary, with an unmistakable lapse into indifference. 'You want to know something about him,' she added, not choosing to indulge Rosamond's indirectness.

'Merely, how you like him.'

'There is no question of liking at present. My liking always wants some little kindness to kindle it. I am not magnanimous enough to like people who speak to me without seeming to see me.'

'Is he so haughty?' said Rosamond, with heightened satisfaction. 'You know that he is of good family?'

'No; he did not give that as a reason.'

'Mary! you are the oddest girl. But what sort of looking man is he? Describe him to me.'

'How can one describe a man? I can give you an inventory: heavy eyebrows, dark eyes, a straight nose, thick dark hair, large solid white hands—and—let me see —oh, an exquisite cambric pocket handkerchief. But you will see him. You know this is about the time of his visits.'

Rosamond blushed a little, but said, meditatively, 'I rather like a haughty manner. I cannot endure a rattling young man.'

'I did not tell you that Mr Lydgate was haughty; but

72

il y en a pour tous les goûts, as little Mamselle used to say, and if any girl can choose the particular sort of conceit she would like, I should think it is you, Rosy.'

'Haughtiness is not conceit; I call Fred conceited.'

Middlemarch, ch. 12

There is no doubt who puts the cards on the table: Mary says what she means and sees through Rosamond's words to what she means. Beauty is important to Rosamond, and so is Lydgate, though she chooses to leave the impression that the opposite is true. This is really a manifestation of her conventionality, opposed throughout to Mary's admittedly rather abrasive directness. With Mary we have 'You know this is about the time of his visits', with Rosamond 'Beauty is of very little consequence . . .': the sort of 'polite' remark that is actually dishonest and insensitive. We might contrast the attitudes towards Miss Morgan: Mary's is tough-minded ('I am not at all sure that everything gets easier as one gets older'), and based on an awareness of another person's reality ('She is interesting to herself'); Rosamond's is dismissive ('uninteresting') and superficial ('not young') and comically pious ('there is religion for a support'). The speech of course reflects the real values she holds, the very opposite of those of her 'tactful' comment about beauty to Mary: it is, after all, the absence of an interesting style which condemns Miss Morgan. There is an extension of this attitude in Mary's impatience with description and Rosamond's interest in it: for Rosamond external qualities matter; for Mary, the haughtiness is what tells. The subject of the passage has really been beauty, true and false, all along.

Rosamond marries Lydgate, and becomes one of the most fascinating child-brides in literature. She is a child-bride because her expectations from life are childishly limitless and her capacity for understanding it similarly limited. Yet she has a terrifying dimension which we do not sense in a figure with whom she might be compared: Dora in Dicken's *David Copperfield*. We might see Dora as a man's version of the bride: dependent, passive, idolizing the male figure so knowing of the world, so beyond her comprehension. George Eliot shows a woman's harsh insight into the destructive potential of dependency, passivity, and hero-worship: the dependency is incessant demand, the passivity quiet inflexibility, and the hero-worship the hero's Procrustean bed. Here they are early in marriage.

22

Presently Rosamond left the piano and seated herself on a chair close to the sofa and opposite her husband's face.

'Is that enough music for you, my lord?' she said, folding her hands before her and putting on a little air of meekness.

'Yes, dear, if you are tired,' said Lydgate, gently, turning his eyes and resting them on her, but not otherwise moving. Rosamond's presence at that moment was perhaps no more than a spoonful brought to the lake, and her woman's instinct in this matter was not dull.

'What is absorbing you?' she said, leaning forward and bringing her face nearer to his.

He moved his hands and placed them gently behind her shoulders.

'I am thinking of a great fellow, who was about as old as I am three hundred years ago, and had already begun a new era in anatomy.'

'I can't guess,' said Rosamond, shaking her head. 'We used to play at guessing historical characters at Mrs Lemon's, but not anatomists.'

'I'll tell you. His name was Vesalius. And the only way he could get to know anatomy as he did, was by going to snatch bodies at night, from graveyards and places of execution.'

'Oh!' said Rosamond, with a look of disgust on her pretty face, 'I am very glad you are not Vesalius. I should have thought he might find some less horrible way than that.'

'No, he couldn't,' said Lydgate, going on too earnestly to take much notice of her answer. 'He could only get a complete skeleton by snatching the whitened bones of a criminal from the gallows, and burying them, and fetching them away by bits secretly, in the dead of night.'

'I hope he is not one of your great heroes,' said Rosamond, half-playfully, half-anxiously, 'else I shall have you getting up in the night to go to St Peter's churchyard. You know how angry you told me the people were about Mrs Goby. You have enemies enough already.'

'So had Vesalius, Rosy. No wonder the medical fogies in Middlemarch are jealous, when some of the greatest doctors living were fierce upon Vesalius because they had believed in Galen, and he showed that Galen was wrong. They called him a liar and a poisonous monster. But the facts of the human frame were on his side; and so he got the better of them.'

'And what happened to him afterwards?' said Rosamond, with some interest.

'Oh, he had a good deal of fighting to the last. And they did exasperate him enough at one time to make him burn a good deal of his work. Then he got shipwrecked just as he was coming from Jerusalem to take a great chair at Padua. He died rather miserably.'

There was a moment's pause before Rosamond said, 'Do you know, Tertius, I often wish you had not been a medical man.'

'Nay, Rosy, don't say that,' said Lydgate, drawing her closer to him. 'That is like saying you wish you had married another man.'

'Not at all; you are clever enough for anything: you might easily have been something else. And your cousins at Quallingham all think that you have sunk below them in your choice of a profession.'

'The cousins at Quallingham may go to the devil!' said Lydgate with scorn. 'It was like their impudence if they said anything of the sort to you.'

'Still,' said Rosamond, 'I do *not* think it is a nice profession, dear.' We know that she had much quiet perseverance in her opinion.

'It is the grandest profession in the world, Rosamond,' said Lydgate, gravely. 'And to say that you love me without loving the medical man in me, is the same sort of thing as to say that you like eating a peach but don't like its flavour. Don't say that again, dear, it pains me.'

'Very well, Doctor Grave-face,' said Rosy, dimpling, 'I will declare in future that I dote on skeletons, and body-snatchers, and bits of things in phials, and quarrels with everybody, that end in your dying miserably.'

'No, no, not so bad as that,' said Lydgate, giving up remonstrance and petting her resignedly.

Middlemarch, ch. 45

This would appear at first glance to be an ordinary conversation between a young married couple but it is really one at cross-purposes, revealing a profound incompatibility. There is an apparent common subject in Vesalius, the anatomical pioneer, and what he represents, but the responses to that subject belong in two different worlds. For Lydgate the world is one of high-minded dedication to the truth in the teeth of orthodox opposition, while for Rosamond the world is rather like that of the orthodox opposition, or the conventional public which serves it. Robbing graves is 'horrible', and medicine is not a 'nice' profession. Her response is an interesting mixture of childlike playfulness, dismissive in a refusal to take seriously ('I will declare in future that I dote on skeletons'), and inflexible conventionality, dismissive in taking its self-interest very seriously ('You have enemies enough already'). The analogy between Lydgate and Vesalius is emphatic: it is made by Lydgate specifically in his reference to the 'medical fogies of Middlemarch', and Rosamond, quick to see a point if not the whole point, makes it too as the subject of conversation shifts back and forth almost interchangeably from Vesalius to her husband. The passage can be seen as marking a stage in the loss of Lydgate's illusions, but it should not be overlooked that it records the disturbance at least of those of Rosamond, as we move from her declaration: 'I am very glad you are not Vesalius', to the worried insight that he might be. The passage as a whole gives a sense of tragic currents working beneath an innocuous surface, epitomized best perhaps in Rosamond's dimpling flirtatiousness as she declares she will dote on those activities that will 'end in your dying miserably'. So he does, though she does not dote.

Of all George Eliot's novels *Daniel Deronda* is the most brilliant in dialogue. One factor behind the brilliance is the novel's heroine, Gwendolen Harleth, certainly the wittiest of George Eliot's heroines. But it is not the only one. Here is one of the most outstanding scenes of the novel, involving not Gwendolen, but more minor characters. Klesmer, a leading European musician who sums up some of the meaning of the theme of art in the novel, has fallen in love with his pupil, Catherine Arrowpoint, daughter of a wealthy family, and of a mother with romantic views on the supreme imperatives of love. It turns out, however, that she does not want her daughter to test her theories.

23

Under the first shock she forgot everything but her anger, and snatched at any phrase that would serve as a weapon.

'If Klesmer has presumed to offer himself to you, your father shall horsewhip him off the premises. Pray, speak, Mr Arrowpoint.'

The father took his cigar from his mouth, and rose to the occasion by saying, 'This will never do, Cath.'

'Do!' cried Mrs Arrowpoint; 'who in their senses ever thought it would do? You might as well say poisoning and strangling will not do. It is a comedy you have got up, Catherine. Else you are mad.'

'I am quite sane and serious, mamma, and Herr Klesmer is not to blame. He never thought of my marrying him. I found out that he loved me, and loving him, I told him I would marry him.'

'Leave that unsaid, Catherine,' said Mrs Arrowpoint, bitterly. 'Every one else will say it for you. You will be a public fable. Every one will say that you must have made the offer to a man who has been paid to come to the house —who is nobody knows what—a gypsy, a Jew, a mere bubble of the earth.'

'Never mind, mamma,' said Catherine, indignant in her turn. 'We all know he is a genius—as Tasso was.'

'Those times were not these, nor is Klesmer Tasso,' said Mrs Arrowpoint, getting more heated. 'There is no sting in *that* sarcasm, except the sting of undutifulness.'

'I am sorry to hurt you, mamma. But I will not give up the happiness of my life to ideas that I don't believe in and customs I have no respect for.'

'You have lost all sense of duty, then? You have forgotten that you are our only child—that it lies with you to place a great property in the right hands?'

'What are the right hands? My grandfather gained the property in trade.'

'Mr Arrowpoint, *will* you sit by and hear this without speaking?'

'I am a gentleman, Cath. We expect you to marry a gentleman,' said the father, exerting himself.

'And a man connected with the institutions of this country,' said the mother. 'A woman in your position has serious duties. Where duty and inclination clash, she must follow duty.'

'I don't deny that,' said Catherine, getting colder in proportion to her mother's heat. 'But one may say very true things and apply them falsely. People can easily take the sacred word duty as a name for what they desire any one else to do.'

'Your parents desire makes no duty for you, then?'

'Yes, within reason. But before I give up the happiness of my life—'

'Catherine, Catherine, it will not be your happiness,' said Mrs Arrowpoint, in her most raven-like tones.

'Well, what seems to me my happiness—before I give it up, I must see some better reason than the wish that I should marry a nobleman, or a man who votes with a party that he may be turned into a nobleman. I feel at liberty to marry the man I love and think worthy, unless some higher duty forbids.'

'And so it does, Catherine, though you are blinded and cannot see it. It is a woman's duty not to lower herself. You are lowering yourself. Mr Arrowpoint, will you tell your daughter what is her duty?'

'You must see, Catherine, that Klesmer is not the man for you,' said Mr Arrowpoint. 'He won't do at the head of estates. He has a deuced foreign look—is an unpractical man.'

'I really can't see what that has to do with it, papa. The land of England has often passed into the hands of foreigners—Dutch soldiers, sons of foreign women of bad character:—if our land were sold tomorrow it would very likely pass into the hands of some foreign merchant on 'Change. It is in everybody's mouth that successful swindlers may buy up half the land in the country. How can I stem that tide?'

'It will never do to argue about marriage, Cath,' said Mr Arrowpoint. 'It's no use getting up the subject like a parliamentary question. We must do as other people do. We must think of the nation and the public good.'

'I can't see any public good concerned here, papa,' said Catherine. 'Why is it to be expected of an heiress that she should carry the property gained in trade into the hands of a certain class? That seems to me a ridiculous mish-mash of superannuated customs and false ambition. I should call it a public evil. People had better make a new sort of public good by changing their ambitions.'

'That is mere sophistry, Catherine,' said Mrs Arrowpoint. 'Because you don't wish to marry a nobleman, you are not obliged to marry a mountebank or a charlatan.'

'I cannot understand the application of such words, mamma.'

'No, I daresay not,' rejoined Mrs Arrowpoint, with significant scorn. 'You have got to a pitch at which we are not likely to understand each other.'

'It can't be done, Cath,' said Mr Arrowpoint, wishing to substitute a better-humoured reasoning for his wife's impetuosity. 'A man like Klesmer can't marry such a property as yours. It can't be done.'

'It certainly will not be done,' said Mrs Arrowpoint, imperiously. 'Where is the man? Let him be fetched.'

Daniel Deronda, ch. 22

There are several sources for the superlative comedy of this passage. Very little of it derives from outside the dialogue in George Eliot's own words ironically placing the situation, as in Mrs Arrowpoint's 'raven-like tones'. Much more comes from the nature of the situation itself, in Mrs Arrowpoint's seeing with horror her literary ideals being carried out in reality by her daughter, or in the more traditional comedy of the irate wife appealing to the husband for masculine support, which is always inadequately forthcoming. But there is a more serious dimension to the comedy which makes it socially satiric as well. The Arrowpoints represent a class assured of the universal validity of its position and values, and we now see their complacent assumptions in shattered confrontation with living ideas. 'What are the right hands? My grandfather gained the property in trade.' And at times these home truths have their own dimension of wit. 'It is in everybody's mouth that successful swindlers may buy up half the country. How can I stem that tide?' Generally speaking, Mrs Arrowpoint is more the satiric object, her husband more the humorous one: she is plainly dishonest with her attitude of outraged virtue ('horsewhip him off the premises') and with her elevated variations on the theme of duty when property is really at stake. With Mr Arrowpoint the technique is rather deflationary: instead of words too grand for the reality, he chooses clichés which are merely dim: 'He won't do at the head of the estates' or 'This will never do, Cath.'

The sophistication of the dialogue in *Daniel Deronda* is a reflection of the sophistication of its characters. True, as with Mr Arrowpoint in the previous extract, George Eliot sometimes comically contrasts class position and influence with the inadequacy of class banalities, but just as frequently the novel shows characters whose speech reflects in imperiousness, wit and range of allusion the habit and environment of command. Such speech is capable of many effects, gaining in subtle precision what is lost in the vigour and directness of the more natural response. (Cf. the debate between Mrs Poyser and Bartle Massey at the opening of this section.) Here is a sample of conversation from the home life of the Grandcourts.

24

But one morning when they were breakfasting, Gwendolen, in a recurrent fit of determination to exercise her old spirit, said, dallying prettily over her prawns without eating them—

'I think of making myself accomplished while we are in town, and having singing lessons.'

'Why?' said Grandcourt, languidly.

'Why?' echoed Gwendolen, playing at sauciness; 'because I can't eat *pâté de foie gras* to make me sleepy, and I can't smoke, and I can't go to the club to make me like to come away again—I want a variety of *ennui*. What would be the most convenient time, when you are busy with your lawyers and people, for me to have lessons from that little Jewess, whose singing is getting all the rage?'

'Whenever you like,' said Grandcourt, pushing away his plate, and leaning back in his chair while he looked at her with his most lizard-like expression, and played with the ears of the tiny spaniel on his lap (Gwendolen had taken a dislike to the dogs because they fawned on him).

Then he said, languidly, 'I don't see why a lady should sing. Amateurs make fools of themselves. A lady can't risk herself in that way in company. And one doesn't want to hear squalling in private.'

'I like frankness: that seems to me a husband's great charm,' said Gwendolen, with her little upward movement of her chin, as she turned her eyes away from his, and lifting a prawn before her, looked at the boiled ingenuousness of its eyes as preferable to the lizard's. 'But,' she added, having devoured her mortification, 'I suppose you don't object to Miss Lapidoth's singing at our party on the 4th? I thought of engaging her. Lady Brackenshaw had her, you know; and the Raymonds, who are very particular about their music. And Mr Deronda, who is a musician himself, and a first-rate judge, says that there is no singing in such good taste as hers for a drawing-room.

I think his opinion is an authority.'

She meant to sling a small stone at her husband in that way.

'It's very indecent of Deronda to go about praising that girl,' said Grandcourt, in a tone of indifference.

'Indecent!' exclaimed Gwendolen, reddening and look-ing at him again, overcome by startled wonder, and unable to reflect on the probable falsity of the phrase— 'to go about praising.'

'Yes; and especially when she is patronized by Lady Mallinger. He ought to hold his tongue about her. Men can see what is his relation to her.'

'Men who judge of others by themselves,' said Gwen-dolen, turning white after her redness, and immediately smitten with a dread of her own words.

'Of course. And a woman should take their judgement —else she is likely to run her head into the wrong place,' said Grandcourt, conscious of using pincers on that white creature. 'I suppose you take Deronda for a saint.'

'Oh dear no!' said Gwendolen, summoning desperately her almost miraculous power of self-control, and speaking in a high hard tone. 'Only a little less of a monster.'

Daniel Deronda, ch. 48

There is a great deal of lazy economy in the speech style, innuendo tending to serve instead of words. When Gwendolen says 'when you are busy with your lawyers and people', the vague 'people' covers the range of Grand-court's activities (or lack of it) as well as suggesting her indifference to them, and Grandcourt's 'indecent' is much more scandalous and nasty in implication than any direct accusation could be. The laziness is more apparent in Grandcourt's speech than in Gwendolen's: he uses short, impatient sentences, just this side of the yawn. It is the style of one used to having his own way, as well as that of one not much interested in anything else. It shows a tendency in a certain kind of languid sophistication:

polish has led to indifference, and indifference to insensitive brutality. 'And one doesn't want to hear squalling in private.' It is Gwendolen who can still delight in the manipulation of words, who is still sensitive to language and hence life: 'I want a variety of *ennui*', or 'I like frankness: that seems to be a husband's great charm.' Always with Gwendolen we sense an inner pressure driving the words, but here the pressure is intensified by Grandcourt's presence. Her wit therefore takes on the quality of a defence: to suggest that Deronda is 'only less of a monster' is a means of momentarily detaching and neutralizing a monstrous reality. The passage gives an extraordinary sense of psychological tensions, which are reflected in speech style generally, but they might also be seen in a more specialized aspect of style, the imagery, both in the speech and in the intervening comment. One might consider the functions of the images, perhaps beginning with the variations on Gwendolen's 'monster'.

Narrative

In this section we turn our attention to George Eliot's management of the most traditional and fundamental of a novelist's skills: story-telling. Of course we cannot consider story as plot, for that implies study of an entire action, impossible to represent in a short extract. But we can consider smaller units which are still narrative, in the sense of embodying a series of events leading to a culmination. These actions are part—sometimes a major part—of plot as a whole. They may be used to create a wide variety of effects, whose range we will attempt to suggest.

Perhaps the most moving and tragic narrative in George Eliot comes in that section of *Adam Bede* describing the wanderings of Hetty Sorrel, who has left the Hall Farm in advanced pregnancy, in a futile search for Arthur Donnithorne, away with the militia and confident that his little adventure is safely over. The section culminates in the birth, abandonment and death of Hetty's child, and it is to lead to her trial and death-sentence for child-murder. Here, early in the journey, Hetty has picked up a ride in a wagon.

25

To lie on the wool-packs, with a cranny left between the curtains of the awning to let in the air, was luxury to Hetty now, and she half slept away the hours till the driver came to ask her if she wanted to get down and have 'some victual'; he himself was going to eat his dinner at this 'public'. Late at night they reached Leicester, and so this second day of Hetty's journey was past. She had spent no money except what she had paid for her food, but she felt that this slow journeying would be intolerable for her another day, and in the morning she found her way to a coach-office to ask about the road to Windsor, and see if it would cost her too much to go part of the distance by coach again. Yes! the distance was too great—the coaches were too dear—she must give them up; but the elderly clerk at the office, touched by her pretty anxious face, wrote down for her the names of the chief places she must pass through. This was the only comfort she got in Leicester, for the men stared at her as she went along the street, and for the first time in her life Hetty wished no one would look at her. She set out walking again; but this day she was fortunate, for she was soon overtaken by a carrier's cart which carried her to Hinckley, and by the help of a return chaise, with a drunken postilion,—who frightened her by driving like Jehu the son of Nimshi, and shouting hilarious remarks at her, twisting himself backwards on his saddle,—she was before night in the heart of woody Warwickshire : but still almost a hundred miles from Windsor, they told her. O what a large world it was, and what hard work for her to find her way in it! She went by mistake to Stratford-on-Avon, finding Stratford set down in her list of places, and then she was told she had come a long way out of the right road. It was not till the fifth day that she got to Stony Stratford. That seems but a slight journey as you look at the map, or remember your own pleasant travels to and from the meadowy banks of the Avon. But how wearily long it was to Hetty! It seemed to her as if this country of flat fields and hedge-rows, and dotted houses, and villages, and market-towns—all so much alike to her indifferent eyes—must have no end, and she must go on wandering among them for ever, waiting tired at toll-gates for some cart to come, and then finding the cart went only a little way—a very little way—to the miller's a mile off perhaps; and she hated going into the public-houses, where she must go to get food and ask questions, because there were always men lounging there, who stared at her and joked her rudely. Her body was very weary too with these days of new fatigue and anxiety; they had made her look more pale and worn than all the time of hidden dread she had gone through at home. When at last she reached Stony Stratford, her impatience and weariness had become too strong for her economical caution; she determined to take the coach for the rest of the way, though it should cost her all her remaining money. She would need nothing at Windsor but to find Arthur. When she had paid her fare for the last coach, she had only a shilling; and as she got down at the sign of the Green Man in Windsor at twelve o'clock in the middle of the seventh day, hungry and faint, the coach-man came up, and begged her to 'remember him'. She put her hand in her pocket, and took out the shilling, but the tears came with the sense of exhaustion and the thought that she was giving away her last means of getting food, which she really required before she could go in search of Arthur. As she held out the shilling, she lifted up her dark tear-filled eyes to the coachman's face and said, 'Can you give me back sixpence?'

'No, no,' he said, gruffly, 'never mind—put the shilling up again.'

Adam Bede, ch. 36

Tragic effect in this passage comes in part from the detail which acts as a correlative both for Hetty's numbed consciousness, and for the larger reality indifferent to it. There is an emphasis on space, distance, impersonality, which is also an emphasis on Hetty's despair, shock, and tragic education. The 'country of flat-fields and hedgerows, and dotted houses, and villages, and market towns' are measures at once of her numbed indifference and the universe indifferent to her; the 'drunken postilion' who frightens her is a representative of both a strange world and one which is estranged. This awareness of a reality whose limits and functions are not those of her desires is new to Hetty, and seems to create new sensitivity to real resources in the comforts of the wool-packs in the opening sentence, or in the possibilities of human sympathy seen in the gesture of the 'elderly clerk at the office' and, most movingly, in the coachman's change of heart about his tip. The resources are tragically inadequate to need, a need which we sense, among other ways, through the rapid pacing of event: it is the pace of time running out. But perhaps the most remarkable feature of all is neither the suggestive use of correlatives nor the narrative pace, but the choice of diction. One might consider its appropriateness for both Hetty's simple nature and for her situation.

The following passage from *The Mill on the Floss* has a particularly psychological emphasis. The child Maggie, having pushed her immaculate cousin Lucy into the mud from jealousy of Tom's interest in her, decides to run away to the gypsies. In the record of her journey we have also the record of her being.

26

Maggie's intentions, as usual, were on a larger scale than Tom had imagined. The resolution that gathered in her mind, after Tom and Lucy had walked away, was not so simple as that of going home. No! She would run away and go to the Gypsies, and Tom should never see her any more. That was by no means a new idea to Maggie; she had been so often told she was like a Gypsy and 'half wild' that when she was miserable it seemed to her the only way of escaping opprobrium, and being entirely in harmony with circumstances would be to live in a little brown tent on the commons; the Gypsies, she considered, would gladly receive her and pay her much respect on account of her superior knowledge. She had once mentioned her views on this point to Tom and suggested that he should stain his face brown and they should run away together; but Tom rejected the scheme with contempt, observing that Gypsies were thieves, and hardly got anything to eat, and had nothing to drive but a donkey. Today, however, Maggie thought her misery had reached a pitch at which Gypsydom was her only refuge, and she rose from her seat on the roots of the tree with the sense that this was a great crisis in her life; she would run straightaway till she came to Dunlow Common, where there would certainly be Gypsies; and cruel Tom, and the rest of her relations who found fault with her, should never see her any more. She thought of her father as she ran along, but she reconciled herself to the idea of parting with him by determining that she would secretly send him a letter by a small Gypsy who would run away without telling where she was and just let him know that she was well and happy and always loved him very much.

Maggie soon got out of breath with running, but by the time Tom got to the pond again, she was at the distance of three long fields and was on the edge of the lane leading to the high-road. She stopped to pant a little, reflecting that running away was not a pleasant thing until one had got quite to the common where the Gypsies were, but her resolution had not abated; she presently passed through the gate into the lane, not knowing where it would lead her, for it was not this way that they came from Dorlcote Mill to Garum Firs, and she felt all the safer for that, because there was no chance of her being overtaken. But she was soon aware, not without trembling, that there were two men coming along the lane in front of her; she had not thought of meeting strangers —she had been too much occupied with the idea of her friends coming after her. The formidable strangers were two shabby-looking men with flushed faces, one of them carrying a bundle on a stick over his shoulder; but to her surprise, while she was dreading their disapprobation as a runaway, the man with the bundle stopped, and in a half-whining, half-coaxing tone asked her if she had a copper to give a poor man. Maggie had a sixpence in her pocket—her uncle Glegg's present—which she immediately drew out and gave this poor man with a polite smile, hoping he would feel very kindly towards her as a generous person. 'That's the only money I've got,' she said apologetically. 'Thank you, little miss,' said the man in a less respectful and grateful tone than Maggie anticipated, and she even observed that he smiled and winked at his companion. She walked on hurriedly, but was aware that the two men were standing still, probably to look after her, and she presently heard them laughing loudly. Suddenly it occurred to her that they might think she was an idiot; Tom had said that her cropped hair made her look like an idiot, and it was too painful an idea to be readily forgotten. Besides, she had no sleeves on, only a cape and a bonnet. It was clear that she was not likely to make a favourable impression on passengers, and she thought she would turn into the fields again; but not on the same side of the lane as before, lest they should still be uncle Pullet's fields. She turned through the first gate that was not locked, and felt a delightful sense of privacy in creeping along by the hedgerows after her recent humiliating encounter. She was used to wandering about the fields by herself and was less timid there than on the high-road. Sometimes she had to climb over high gates, but that was a small evil; she was getting out of reach very fast, and she should probably soon come within sight of Dunlow Common, or at least of some other common, for she had heard her father say that you couldn't go very far without coming to a common. She hoped so, for she was getting rather tired and hungry, and until she reached the Gypsies there was no definite prospect of bread and butter. It was still broad daylight, for aunt Pullet, retaining the early habits of the Dodson family, took tea at half-past four by the sun and at five by the kitchen clock; so, though it was nearly an hour since Maggie started, there was no gathering gloom on the fields to remind her that the night would come. Still, it seemed to her that she had been walking a very great distance indeed, and it was really surprising that the common did not come within sight. Hitherto she had been in the rich parish of Garum, where there was a great deal of pasture-land, and she had only seen one labourer at a distance. That was fortunate in some respects, as labourers might be too ignorant to understand the propriety of her wanting to go to Dunlow Common; yet it would have been better if she could have met someone who would tell her the way without wanting to know anything about her private business. At last, however, the green fields came to an end, and Maggie found herself looking through the bars of a gate into a lane with a wide margin of grass on each side of it. She had never seen such a wide lane before, and without her knowing why, it gave her the impression that the common could not be far off; perhaps it was because she saw a donkey with a log to his foot feeding on the grassy margin, for she had seen a donkey with that pitiable encumbrance on Dunlow Common when she had been across it in her father's gig. She crept through the bars of the gate and walked on with new spirit, though not without haunting images of Apollyon, and a highwayman with a pistol, and a blinking dwarf in yellow, with a mouth from ear to ear, and other miscellaneous dangers. For poor little Maggie had at once the timidity of an active imagination and the daring that comes from overmastering impulse. She had rushed into the adventure of seeking her unknown kindred, the Gypsies; and now she was in this strange lane, she

hardly dared look on one side of her, lest she should see
the diabolical blacksmith in his leathern apron grinning at
her with arms akimbo. It was not without a leaping of the
heart that she caught sight of a small pair of bare legs
sticking up, feet uppermost, by the side of a hillock; they
seemed something hideously preternatural—a diabolical
kind of fungus; for she was too much agitated at the first
glance to see the ragged clothes and the dark shaggy head
attached to them. It was a boy asleep, and Maggie trotted
along faster and more lightly, lest she should wake him; it
did not occur to her that he was one of her friends the
Gypsies, who in all probability would have very genial
manners. But the fact was so, for at the next bend in the
lane, Maggie actually saw the little semicircular black
tent with the blue smoke rising before it which was to be
her refuge from all the blighting obloquy that had pursued
her in civilized life. She even saw a tall female figure
by the column of smoke—doubtless the Gypsy mother,
who provided the tea and other groceries; it was astonish-
ing to herself that she did not feel more delighted. But
it was startling to find the Gypsies in a lane, after all, and
not on a common; indeed, it was rather disappointing; for
a mysterious illimitable common, where there were
sand-pits to hide in and one was out of everybody's reach,
had always made part of Maggie's picture of Gypsy life.
She went on, however, and thought with some comfort
that Gypsies most likely knew nothing about idiots, so
there was no danger of their falling into the mistake of
setting her down at the first glance as an idiot.

The Mill on the Floss, Bk. I, ch. 11

The prose of this passage is like much in *The Mill on
the Floss*: direct, natural, and extraordinarily rich in
effect. It is just as subtle as the more imagistic and
symbolic prose of *Middlemarch* and *Daniel Deronda*, and
harder to analyse. The reason lies in its very naturalness,
its 'unliterary' quality. There is no pattern of metaphor
which may be abstracted to give a shorthand equivalent

of meaning. We have to look at parts of the passage more than at parts of the language to see a structural pattern, and even that is subdued and much qualified. The basic rhythm is that of Maggie's consciousness: a sense of rejection alternating with a compensatory sense of pre-eminence, the sense of being unloved alternating with the sense of being universally loved. Sometimes these feelings are given through Maggie's memories and hopes: Tom is 'cruel', her relations 'find fault with her', or 'the Gypsies . . . would gladly receive her and pay her much respect'. More frequently they are implicit in her reaction to the immediate environment of the journey where, again and again, the reality is shown to be inadequate to her demands on it, just as the love she has received is inade-quate to her need of it. Thus she finds, as she escapes, that running away was not, after all, 'such a pleasant thing', then meets the two men and finds her charity rewarded with 'a less respectful and grateful tone' than anticipated as well as by the laugh which cuts so deep. Then, going on, she finds that she is not immune to hunger, that the common she seeks seems surprisingly distant, and that the gypsies, anyway, have not chosen to camp there, but on an un-romantic lane.

Yet this pattern is much qualified. Hope and disappoint-ment are only the main feelings among others which include, for example, delight, discontent, sympathy, and notably the fear which is also displaced guilt. It is con-veyed in the images of the hostile 'Apollyon, and a high-wayman with a pistol, and a blinking dwarf in yellow, with a mouth from ear to ear, and other miscellaneous dangers' and later in the 'diabolical blacksmith' and the frightening pair of legs of the real boy asleep. Nor are all the references to the past unpleasant: her father is not of the company rejecting her, and 'wandering about the fields' and 'bread and butter' are among the things explicitly or implicitly part of it. And, overall, there is the controlling authorial tone of sympathy and indulgent amusement which keeps the childhood crisis in perspective.

Silas Marner is frequently compared to a parable or fairy-tale. The story of an embittered miser who is restored to human contacts by love for a child, it represents a kind of realistic writing which has strong symbolic overtones. The following passage records Marner's discovery of the child, shortly after his hoard of gold has been stolen. The 'Lantern Yard' of the passage is Silas' former home town, from which he had exiled himself years before, bitter at a betrayal by a friend which also seemed a betrayal by God.

27

This morning he had been told by some of his neighbours that it was New Year's Eve, and that he must sit up and hear the old year rung out and the new rung in, because that was good luck, and might bring his money back again. This was only a friendly Raveloe way of jesting with the half-crazy oddities of a miser, but it had perhaps helped to throw Silas into a more than usually excited state. Since the oncoming of twilight he had opened his door again and again, though only to shut it immediately at seeing all distance veiled by the falling snow. But the last time he opened it the snow had ceased, and the clouds were parting here and there. He stood and listened, and gazed for a long while—there was really something on the road coming towards him then, but he caught no sign of it; and the stillness and the wide trackless snow seemed to narrow his solitude, and touched his yearning with the chill of despair. He went in again, and put his right hand on the latch of the door to close it—

but he did not close it: he was arrested, as he had been already since his loss, by the invisible wand of catalepsy, and stood like a graven image, with wide but sightless eyes, holding open his door, powerless to resist either the good or evil that might enter there.

When Marner's sensibility returned, he continued the action which had been arrested, and closed his door, unaware of the chasm in his consciousness, unaware of any intermediate change, except that the light had grown dim, and that he was chilled and faint. He thought he had been too long standing at the door and looking out. Turning towards the hearth, where the two logs had fallen apart, and sent forth only a red, uncertain glimmer, he seated himself on his fireside chair, and was stooping to push his logs together, when, to his blurred vision, it seemed as if there were gold on the floor in front of the hearth. Gold!—his own gold—brought back to him as mysteriously as it had been taken away! He felt his heart begin to beat violently, and for a few moments he was unable to stretch out his hand and grasp the restored treasure. The heap of gold seemed to glow and get larger beneath his agitated gaze. He leaned forward at last, and stretched forth his hand; but instead of the hard coin with the familiar resisting outline, his fingers encountered soft, warm curls. In utter amazement, Silas fell on his knees and bent his head low to examine the marvel: it was a sleeping child—a round, fair thing, with soft yellow rings all over its head. Could this be his little sister come back to him in a dream—his little sister whom he had carried about in his arms for a year before she died, when he was a small boy without shoes or stockings? That was the first thought that darted across Silas's blank wonderment. *Was* it a dream? He rose to his feet again, pushed his logs together, and, throwing on some dried leaves and sticks, raised a flame; but the flame did not disperse the vision—it only lit up more distinctly the little round form of the child and its shabby clothing. It was very much like his little sister. Silas sank into his chair powerless, under the double presence of an inexplicable surprise and a hurrying influx of memories. How and when had the child come in without his knowledge? He had never been beyond the door. But along with that question, and almost thrusting it away, there was a vision of the old home and the old streets leading to Lantern Yard—and within that vision another, of the thoughts which had been present with him in those far-off scenes. The thoughts were strange to him now, like old friendships impossible to revive; and yet he had a dreamy feeling that this child was somehow a message come to him from that far-off life : it stirred fibres that had never been moved in Raveloe —old quiverings of tenderness—old impressions of awe at the presentiment of some Power presiding over his life; for his imagination had not yet extricated itself from the sense of mystery in the child's sudden presence, and had formed no conjectures of ordinary means by which the event could have been brought about.

Silas Marner, ch. 12

The passage is largely built on symbolic antitheses which are variations on the central antithesis of 'good and evil' specifically suggested at the close of the first paragraph. These antitheses suggest a simpler and more providential universe than the one we know : its ways are inexplicable but its meaning clear, unlike our rationalist's universe whose meaning is obscure but processes explicable. The antitheses are seen, for example, in the contrast between old and new year, good and bad luck, the warmth of the fire and the cold outside, the death-like trance and the life of Silas's reactivated memory, and, most centrally, the gold of the hair of the living child and the inanimate metallic gold he has lost. Throughout the emphasis is on renewal, on life conquering death : the new year replaces the old, the child the gold, memories and sympathy the 'graven image' of Silas in the trance. The combination of fortuitous coincidences leading to the child's discovery is unusual in George Eliot's fiction, where happiness is usually earned through moral struggle, though it is appropriate to the fairy-tale convention. However the author carefully provides a rational explanation for everything that happens, reserving the sense of mystery ultimately embodied in 'awe at some Power presiding over his life' for Silas, and not the reader.

Middlemarch, more than any other novel of George Eliot, is one of subdued effects, one which attempts, in a Wordsworthian manner, to see significances in material which might be ordinarily overlooked. We see one manifestation of this concern in the novel's emphasis on ordinary domestic life, whose crises and triumphs never reach the history books. Here is a typical episode. Casaubon has been given an uncertain prognosis for a heart condition which has recently troubled him, and Dorothea's gesture of sympathy—a simple and moving linking of her arm with his—has been unresponsively and coldly received. Here we see her vigil over her rage.

28

The sun was low when Dorothea was thinking that she would not go down again, but would send a message to her husband saying that she was not well and preferred remaining up-stairs. She had never deliberately allowed her resentment to govern her in this way before, but she believed now that she could not see him again without telling him the truth about her feeling, and she must wait till she could do it without interruption. He might wonder and be hurt at her message. It was good that he should wonder and be hurt. Her anger said, as anger is apt to say, that God was with her—that all heaven, though it were crowded with spirits watching them, must be on her side. She had determined to ring her bell, when there came a rap at the door.

Mr Casaubon had sent to say that he would have his dinner in the library. He wished to be quite alone this evening, being much occupied.

'I shall not dine, then, Tantripp.'

'Oh, madam, let me bring you a little something?'

'No; I am not well. Get everything ready in my dressing-room, but pray do not disturb me again.'

Dorothea sat almost motionless in her meditative struggle, while the evening slowly deepened into night. But the struggle changed continually, as that of a man who begins with a movement towards striking and ends with conquering his desire to strike. The energy that would animate a crime is not more than is wanted to inspire a resolved submission, when the noble habit of the soul reasserts itself. That thought with which Dorothea had gone out to meet her husband—her conviction that he had been asking about the possible arrest of all his work, and that the answer must have wrung his heart, could not be long without rising beside the image of him, like a shadowy monitor looking at her anger with sad remonstrance. It cost her a litany of pictured sorrows and of silent cries that she might be the mercy for those sorrows—but the resolved submission did come; and when the house was still, and she knew that it was near the time when Mr Casaubon habitually went to rest, she opened her door gently and stood outside in the darkness waiting for his coming up-stairs with a light in his hand. If he did not come soon she thought that she would go down and even risk incurring another pang. She would never again expect anything else. But she did hear the library door open, and slowly the light advanced up the staircase without noise from the footsteps on the carpet. When her husband stood opposite to her, she saw that his face was more haggard. He started slightly on seeing her, and she looked up at him beseechingly, without speaking.

'Dorothea!' he said, with a gentle surprise in his tone. 'Were you waiting for me?'

'Yes, I did not like to disturb you.'

'Come, my dear, come. You are young, and need not to extend your life by watching.'

When the kind quiet melancholy of that speech fell on Dorothea's ears, she felt something like the thankfulness that might well up in us if we had narrowly escaped hurting a lamed creature. She put her hand into her husband's, and they went along the broad corridor together.

Middlemarch, ch. 42

This is narrative of inner rather than external event, of moral crisis and the movement of feeling. It is a characteristic movement in George Eliot's fiction, from self-absorption to sympathy, as in the period between sundown and later night we trace the progress from Dorothea's conviction of the absolute justice of her rage—'God was with her'—to the 'resolved submission' of the close. Within the overall moving summary that gives us a concentrated version of Dorothea's struggle one senses touches of that diffuseness which sometimes blurs George Eliot's rendering of a character's inner life, but there can be no reservations about the close of the section. Here the hand is sure, underwriting rather than overwriting, as Dorothea's silent gaze at her husband's haggard face, his new tenderness in the quiet exchange, and the moving, final action, evoke the preceding context and echo a larger context of human love, while the solitary authorial comment about Dorothea's thankfulness places the scene and her struggle in terms of the essential moral issue.

Though *Middlemarch* is primarily a novel of 'normal' life, it is too rich to be easily and completely so defined. Certainly there is one sensational event in *Middlemarch*: a murder. We should notice, however, that the treatment of this murder is unsensational: the focus is on the psychology of the killer, and the means of murder is itself subtle: the deliberate neglect of proper medical treatment rather than poison, gun, or axe. The killer is the banker

Bulstrode, sanctimoniously respectable, a man who has made his fortune shadily, but prospers in the sun. He is not, we are told, a 'coarse hypocrite' but rather one whose conscience is frequently troubled—though always finally reassured—by attempts to square his wrong-doing with his religious beliefs. He murders the only one who knows the full truth about his past, a man called Raffles, who is now under his care in a state of alcoholic but embarrassingly garrulous delirium, by neglecting the prescription instructions left by Lydgate and applying more orthodox but fatal treatment.

29

At six o'clock, Raffles, having had only fitful perturbed snatches of sleep, from which he waked with fresh restlessness and perpetual cries that he was sinking away, Bulstrode began to administer the opium according to Lydgate's directions. At the end of half an hour or more he called Mrs Abel and told her that he found himself unfit for further watching. He must now consign the patient to her care; and he proceeded to repeat to her Lydgate's directions as to the quantity of each dose. Mrs Abel had not before known anything of Lydgate's prescriptions; she had simply prepared and brought whatever Bulstrode ordered, and had done what he pointed out to her. She began now to ask what else she should do besides administering the opium.

'Nothing at present, except the offer of the soup or the soda-water : you can come to me for further directions. Unless there is any important change, I shall not come into the room again to-night. You will ask your husband for help, if necessary. I must go to bed early.'

'You've much need, sir, I'm sure,' said Mrs Abel, 'and to take something more strengthening than what you've done.'

Bulstrode went away now without anxiety as to what Raffles might say in his raving, which had taken on a muttering incoherence not likely to create any dangerous belief. At any rate he must risk this. He went down into the wainscoted parlour first, and began to consider whether he would not have his horse saddled and go home by the moonlight, and give up caring for earthly consequences. Then, he wished that he had begged Lydgate to come again that evening. Perhaps he might deliver a different opinion, and think that Raffles was getting into a less hopeful state. Should he send for Lydgate? If Raffles were really getting worse, and slowly dying, Bulstrode felt that he could go to bed and sleep in gratitude to Providence. But was he worse? Lydgate might come and simply say that he was going on as he expected, and predict that he would by-and-by fall into a good sleep, and get well. What was the use of sending for him? Bulstrode shrank from that result. No ideas or opinions could hinder him from seeing the one probability to be, that Raffles recovered would be just the same man as before, with his strength as a tormentor renewed, obliging him to drag away his wife to spend her years apart from her friends and native place, carrying an alienating suspicion against him in her heart.

He had sat an hour and a half in this conflict by the fire-light only, when a sudden thought made him rise and light the bed-candle, which he had brought down with him. The thought was, that he had not told Mrs Abel when the doses of opium must cease.

He took hold of the candlestick, but stood motionless for a long while. She might already have given him more than Lydgate had prescribed. But it was excusable in him, that he should forget part of an order, in his present wearied condition. He walked up-stairs, candle in hand, not knowing whether he should straightway enter his own room and go to bed, or turn to the patient's room and rectify his omission. He paused in the passage, with his face turned towards Raffles's room, and he could hear him moaning and murmuring. He was not asleep, then,

Who could know that Lydgate's prescription would not be better disobeyed than followed, since there was still no sleep?

He turned into his own room. Before he had quite undressed, Mrs Abel rapped at the door; he opened it an inch, so that he could hear her speak low.

'If you please, sir, should I have no brandy nor nothing to give the poor creetur? He feels sinking away, and nothing else will he swaller—and but little strength in it, if he did—only the opium. And he says more and more he's sinking down through the earth.'

To her surprise, Mr Bulstrode did not answer. A struggle was going on within him.

'I think he must die for want o' support, if he goes on in that way. When I nursed my poor master, Mr Robisson, I had to give him port-wine and brandy constant, and a big glass at a time,' added Mrs Abel with a touch of remonstrance in her tone.

But again Mr Bulstrode did not answer immediately, and she continued, 'It's not a time to spare when people are at death's door, nor would you wish it, sir, I'm sure. Else I should give him our own bottle o' rum as we keep by us. But a sitter-up so as you've been, and doing everything as laid in your power—'

Here a key was thrust through the inch of doorway, and Mr Bulstrode said huskily, 'That is the key of the wine-cooler. You will find plenty of brandy there.'

Early in the morning—about six—Mr Bulstrode rose and spent some time in prayer. Does any one suppose that private prayer is necessarily candid—necessarily goes to the roots of action! Private prayer is inaudible speech, and speech is representative: who can represent himself just as he is, even in his own reflections? Bulstrode had not yet unravelled in his thought the confused promptings of the last four-and-twenty hours.

He listened in the passage, and could hear hard stertorous breathing. Then he walked out in the garden, and looked at the early rime on the grass and fresh spring leaves. When he re-entered the house, he felt startled at the sight of Mrs Abel.

'How is your patient—asleep, I think?' he said, with an attempt at cheerfulness in his tone.

'He's gone very deep, sir,' said Mrs Abel. 'He went off gradual between three and four o'clock. Would you please to go and look at him? I thought it no harm to leave him. My man's gone afield, and the little girl's seeing to the kettles.'

Bulstrode went up. At a glance he knew that Raffles was not in the sleep which brings revival, but in the sleep which streams deeper and deeper into the gulf of death.

He looked round the room and saw a bottle with some brandy in it, and the almost empty opium phial. He put the phial out of sight, and carried the brandy-bottle downstairs with him, locking it again in the wine-cooler.

Middlemarch, ch. 70

Event here has its fundamental appeal in the tense stages leading to the murder, but the narrative also reveals the self-deluding mind of the murderer which determines them. What looks like an innocent act, the assignation of the care of Raffles to Mrs Abel, and what looks like a less innocent inner debate about calling Lydgate to the case, are *both* revealed to be unconscious and homicidal choices. The assignation provides Bulstrode with the opportunity to forget instruction about a vital part of the treatment, the cessation of the doses of opium, and the debate by the fire fills time so that he will not remember—until too late—that he forgot. Bulstrode finds an excuse: he was tired. But the true reason becomes transparent almost immediately in his hesitation about correcting the mistake until he can grab the straw: 'Who could know that Lydgate's prescription would not be better disobeyed than followed, since there was still no sleep?' And, finally, it becomes transparent even to Bulstrode himself. There are no rationalizations when Mrs Abel asks for some brandy for the patient (absolutely prohibited by Lydgate), because none are possible.

We hear nothing of Bulstrode's inner struggle. Throughout the passage there has been an emphasis on silence and quiet vigil: in the waiting by the fire, the setting at night, the stupor of the patient, only broken by the instructions for treatment and Raffles' incoherent mutters, but now, close to the decision, we are even shut off from the inner world. What remains is a matter-of-fact surface which resonates with the appalling and unstated, especially in Mrs Abel's rambling, semi-literate request, whose normality and innocence paradoxically remind us of a context which is not. In the morning there is again normality, with the same kind of suggestiveness, but some additional qualities as well. Bulstrode feels relaxed and relatively free of tension: 'he walked out in the garden and looked at the early rime on the grass and fresh spring leaves', sensing in its renewal of morning and spring renewal for him as well. But we know that it is no renewal for Raffles, and therefore that its reassurance is delusory and reality indifferent. It is Bulstrode's symbol, not the author's. Then, after the conversation with Mrs Abel, and the glance at the dying man comes the final act as Bulstrode tidies up: 'He put the phial out of sight, and carried the brandy-bottle down-stairs with him, locking it again in the wine-cooler'. The details suggest completion and finality, but they are again ironic. Bulstrode's management of his immorality has always involved the concealment of external evidence and the 'locking up' of unfortunate memories on the false assumption that invisibility may be equated with non-existence. He treats his own history the way the rulers of the world-states in Orwell's *1984* treat political history.

What is usually called the 'Jewish half' of *Daniel Deronda* is the story of a destiny unusual in George Eliot in that it seems to be directed by other than ordinary causes. A series of coincidences leads the hero Deronda to the discovery that he is Jewish, a discovery presented in terms of auspicious liberation. Here is one of the key events: a chance encounter between Deronda and Mordecai, an aging Jew of prophetic vision who knows, without any evidence, what the hero is and is to be.

30

When the wherry was approaching Blackfriars Bridge, where Deronda meant to land, it was half-past four, and the grey day was dying gloriously, its western clouds all broken into narrowing purple strata before a wide-spreading saffron clearness, which in the sky had a monumental calm, but on the river, with its changing objects, was reflected as a luminous movement, the alternate flash of ripples or currents, the sudden glow of the brown sail, the passage of laden barges from blackness into colour, making an active response to that brooding glory.

Feeling well heated by this time, Deronda gave up the oar and drew over him again his Inverness cape. As he lifted up his head while fastening the topmost button, his eyes caught a well-remembered face looking towards him over the parapet of the bridge—brought out by the western light into startling distinctness and brilliancy—an illuminated type of bodily emaciation and spiritual eagerness. It was the face of Mordecai, who also, in his watch towards the west, had caught sight of the advancing boat, and had kept it fast within his gaze, at first simply because it was advancing, then with a recovery of impressions that made him quiver as with a presentiment, till at last the nearing figure lifted up its face towards him—the face of his visions—and then immediately, with white uplifted hand, beckoned again and again.

For Deronda, anxious that Mordecai should recognize and await him, had lost no time before signalling, and the answer came straightway. Mordecai lifted his cap and waved it—feeling in that moment that his inward prophecy was fulfilled. Obstacles, incongruities, all melted into the sense of completion with which his soul was flooded by this outward satisfaction of his longing. His exultation was not widely different from that of the experimenter, bending over the first stirrings of change that correspond to what in the fervour of concentrated prevision his thought has fore-shadowed. The prefigured friend had come from the golden background, and had signalled to him: this actually was: the rest was to be.

In three mintues Deronda had landed, had paid his boatman, and was joining Mordecai, whose instinct it was to stand perfectly still and wait for him.

'I was very glad to see you standing here,' said Deronda, 'for I was intending to go on to the book-shop and look for you again. I was there yesterday—perhaps they mentioned it to you?'

'Yes,' said Mordecai; 'that was the reason I came to the bridge.'

This answer, made with simple gravity, was startlingly mysterious to Deronda. Were the peculiarities of this man really associated with any sort of mental alienation, according to Cohen's hint?

'You knew nothing of my being at Chelsea?' he said after a moment.

'No: but I expected you to come down the river. I have been waiting for you these five years.' Mordecai's deep-sunk eyes were fixed on those of the friend who had at last arrived, with a look of affectionate dependence, at once pathetic and solemn. Deronda's sensitiveness was not the less responsive because he could not but believe that this strangely-disclosed relation was founded on an illusion.

Daniel Deronda, ch. 40

This is narrative working to suggest higher forces controlling human and perhaps especially racial destiny than are rationally explicable. The technique is mainly one in which symbol is made to dwarf the significance of argument. Deronda has apparently gone down river casually but it was really to keep an appointment, as not only Mordecai's fervid conviction but also its endorsement from the glorious sunset illuminating his countenance and transforming the river and its human activity makes clear. Such a symbolic frame would belittle even persuasive objection, and Deronda's is weak. One might ask whether the supporting reference to the 'experimenter' in the third paragraph is consistent with the theme of the passage.

Narrative implies event, which in turn implies process and change. It follows that the absence of event may itself be significant, suggesting the frustration or end of any possible action. Damnation in Coleridge's 'Ancient Mariner' is suggested in part by the isolation of a motionless ship on the ocean; here is a similar damnation in *Daniel Deronda*, as Gwendolen goes yachting with her husband on the Mediterranean. 'Mr Lush' is his secretary.

31

What had she to complain of? The yacht was of the prettiest; the cabin fitted up to perfection, smelling of cedar, soft-cushioned, hung with silk, expanded with mirrors; the crew such as suited an elegant toy, one of them having even ringlets, as well as a bronze complexion and fine teeth; and Mr Lush was not there, for he had taken his way back to England as soon as he had seen all and everything on board. Moreover, Gwendolen herself liked the sea: it did not make her ill; and to observe the rigging of the vessel and forecast the necessary adjustments was a sort of amusement that might have gratified her activity and enjoyment of imaginary rule; the weather was fine, and they were coasting southward, where even the rain-furrowed, heat-cracked clay becomes gem-like with purple shadows, and where one may float between blue and blue in an open-eyed dream that the world has done with sorrow.

But what can still that hunger of the heart which sickens the eye for beauty, and makes sweet-scented ease an oppression? What sort of Moslem paradise would quiet the terrible fury of moral repulsion and cowed resistance which, like an eating pain intensifying into torture, concentrates the mind in that poisonous misery? While Gwendolen, throned on her cushions at evening, and beholding the glory of sea and sky softening as if with boundless love around her, was hoping that Grandcourt in his march up and down was not going to pause near her, not going to look at her or speak to her, some woman under a smoky sky, obliged to consider the price of eggs in arranging her dinner, was listening for the music of a footstep that would remove all risk from her foretaste of joy; some couple, bending, cheek by cheek, over a bit of work done by the one and delighted in by the other, were reckoning the earnings that would make them rich enough for a holiday among the furze and heather.

Had Grandcourt the least conception of what was going on in the breast of this wife? He conceived that she did not love him: but was that necessary? She was under his power, and he was not accustomed to soothe himself, as some cheerfully-disposed persons are, with the conviction that he was very generally and justly beloved. But what lay quite away from his conception was, that she could have any special repulsion for him personally. How could she? He himself knew what personal repulsion was —nobody better: his mind was much furnished with a sense of what brutes his fellow-creatures were, both masculine and feminine; what odious familiarities they had, what smirks, what modes of flourishing their handkerchiefs, what costume, what lavender-water, what bulging eyes, and what foolish notions of making themselves agreeable by remarks which were not wanted. In this critical view of mankind there was an affinity between him and Gwendolen before their marriage, and we know that she had been attractingly wrought upon by the refined negations he presented to her. Hence he understood her repulsion for Lush. But how was he to understand or conceive her present repulsion for Henleigh Grandcourt? Some men bring themselves to believe, and not merely maintain, the non-existence of an external world; a few others believe themselves objects of repulsion to a woman without being told so in plain language. But Grandcourt did not belong to this eccentric body of thinkers. He had all his life had reason to take a flattering view of his own attractiveness, and to place himself in fine antithesis to the men who, he saw at once, must be revolting to a woman of taste. He had no idea of a moral repulsion, and could not have believed, if he had been told it, that there may be a resentment and disgust which will gradually make beauty more detestable than ugliness, through exasperation at that outward virtue in which hateful things can flaunt themselves or find a supercilious advantage.

How, then, could Grandcourt divine what was going on in Gwendolen's breast?

For their behaviour to each other scandalized no observer—not even the foreign maid warranted against sea-sickness; nor Grandcourt's own experienced valet; still less the picturesque crew, who regarded them as a model couple in high life. Their companionship consisted chiefly in a well-bred silence. Grandcourt had no humorous observations at which Gwendolen could refuse to smile, no chit-chat to make small occasions of dispute. He was perfectly polite in arranging an additional garment over her when needful, and in handing her any object that he perceived her to need, and she could not fall into the vulgarity of accepting or rejecting such politeness rudely.

Grandcourt put up his telescope and said, 'There's a plantation of sugar-canes at the foot of that rock: should you like to look?'

Gwendolen said, 'Yes, please,' remembering that she

must try and interest herself in sugar-canes as something outside her personal affairs. Then Grandcourt would walk up and down and smoke for a long while, pausing occasionally to point out a sail on the horizon, and at last would seat himself and look at Gwendolen with his narrow, immovable gaze, as if she were part of the complete yacht; while she, conscious of being looked at, was exerting her ingenuity not to meet his eyes. At dinner he would remark that the fruit was getting stale, and they must put in somewhere for more; or, observing that she did not drink the wine, he asked her if she would like any other kind better. A lady was obliged to respond to these things suitably; and even if she had not shrunk from quarrelling on other grounds, quarrelling with Grandcourt was impossible: she might as well have made angry remarks to a dangerous serpent ornamentally coiled in her cabin without invitation. And what sort of dispute could a woman of any pride and dignity begin on a yacht?

Daniel Deronda, ch. 54

There are two modes of writing evident in this passage. It opens and closes with a largely external and descriptive presentation of the yacht and the activities on it, while in between it gives us an analytic rendering of the feelings of Grandcourt and Gwendolen about themselves and each other. The analytic presentation is carefully underlined as a comment on the descriptive: what meets the eye in an elegant and idle life in luxurious surroundings gives no clue to the reality of Gwendolen's torment and Grandcourt's vast and terrifying self-complacency. Yet the descriptive presentation has its own kind of irony: if it cannot suggest psychological implications, it can suggest the social. The yachting represents a way of life which is more style than substance. There is something ludicrous in an 'elegant toy' whose outfitting includes such attention to detail as a crew member with 'ringlets . . . a bronze complexion and fine teeth'. The reality of life on board is the triviality suggested in views of sugar-canes and conversation about stale fruit, or the boredom of the 'well-bred silence'. And the situation of the boat, alone at sea, underlines the main point: the way of life involves an isolation from purposeful aims and the general life of mankind. Its pointlessness is emphasized in several ways —in, for example, ironic images like 'throned on her cushions'—but perhaps the most subtle of these is the summary nature of the description: many days can be dealt with as one because they are all the same.

Select Bibliography

I WORKS OF GEORGE ELIOT

A. *Original Editions.* I have not included the two translations (the third, of Spinoza's *Ethics*, was never published), nor the magazine publication of individual poems and essays.

Scenes of Clerical Life, 2 vols., Edinburgh, 1858. Originally printed in *Blackwood's Magazine*, January to November 1857.
Adam Bede, 3 vols., Edinburgh, 1859.
The Mill on the Floss, 3 vols., Edinburgh, 1860.
Silas Marner: The Weaver of Raveloe, Edinburgh, 1861.
Romola, 3 vols., Smith and Elder, London, 1863. Originally printed in the *Cornhill Magazine*, July 1862 to August 1863.
Felix Holt: The Radical, 3 vols., Edinburgh, 1866.
The Spanish Gypsy: A Poem, Edinburgh, 1868.
Middlemarch: A Study of Provincial Life, 4 vols., Edinburgh, 1871-72. First published in eight parts.
The Legend of Jubal and Other Poems, Edinburgh, 1874.
Daniel Deronda, 4 vols., Edinburgh, 1876. First published in eight parts.
Impressions of Theophrastus Such, Edinburgh, 1879. Essays.
Essays and Leaves from a Note-book, Edinburgh, 1884.
Quarry for Middlemarch, ed. Anna Theresa Kitchel, Berkeley, 1950. George Eliot's notebook for the novel.
Haight, Gordon. *The George Eliot Letters*, 7 vols., Yale University Press, 1954-56.
Pinney, Thomas. *Essays of George Eliot*, Routledge, London, 1963. A useful selection from the early critical articles.

B. *Texts.* There is no fully edited text of George Eliot's works, and no modern collected edition. The standard edition is the cabinet edition (20 vols.), Edinburgh, 1878-80, the last issued in the author's lifetime. It is scarce. The following are modern texts, English and American, most of them with useful critical introductions.

Adam Bede, intr. F. R. Leavis, New English Library (Signet Classics), London.

Adam Bede, intr. Gordon Haight, Rinehart, New York.

The Mill on the Floss, New English Library (Signet Classics), London.

The Mill on the Floss, ed. Gordon Haight, Houghton-Mifflin (Riverside editions), Cambridge, Mass.

Silas Marner, ed. Q. D. Leavis, Penguin (Penguin English Library), Harmondsworth, Middlesex.

Silas Marner, intr. Jerome Thale, Rinehart, New York.

Romola, Dent (Everyman's Library), London.

Felix Holt, Panther Books, London.

Middlemarch, ed. W. J. Harvey, Penguin (Penguin English Library), Harmondsworth, Middlesex.

Middlemarch, ed. Gordon Haight, Houghton-Mifflin (Riverside editions), Cambridge, Mass.

Daniel Deronda, ed. Barbara Hardy, Penguin (Penguin English Library), Harmondsworth, Middlesex.

Daniel Deronda, intr. F. R. Leavis, Harper (Harper Torchbooks), New York.

Everyman's Library also carries all the other novels; World's Classics *Romola*, *Middlemarch*, *Silas Marner*, and *The Mill on the Floss*; Signet Classics also *Middlemarch* and *Silas Marner*. The only modern edition of *Scenes of Clerical Life* appears to be one published by Thomas Nelson and Sons, London.

II SECONDARY SOURCES

A. *Biographical and Textual*

BEATY, JEROME, *'Middlemarch' from Notebook to Novel*, Urbana, 1960. A close study of the textual changes and their significance in the novel.

HAIGHT, GORDON S., *George Eliot: A Biography*, Oxford University Press, 1968. The definitive modern biography.

B. *Critical*

BENNETT, JOAN, *George Eliot: Her Mind and Art*, Cambridge University Press, 1948. Unlike works such as W. J. Harvey's *Art of George Eliot* and Barbara Hardy's *The Novels of George Eliot*

SELECT BIBLIOGRAPHY

listed below, has chapters on individual novels. The best introduction.

DAICHES, DAVID, *Middlemarch*, Edward Arnold, London, 1963. An introduction to the novel.

HAIGHT, GORDON S., *A Century of George Eliot Criticism*, Methuen, London, 1966. An indispensible introduction to George Eliot criticism.

HARDY, BARBARA, *The Novels of George Eliot: A Study in Form*, Athlone Press, London, 1959. A closely written and stimulating study of structural patterns which is probably the best critical study of George Eliot.

HARDY, BARBARA (ed.), *Middlemarch*, Athlone Press, London, 1967. An Anglo-American collection of highly specialized critical and scholarly essays.

HARVEY, W. J., *The Art of George Eliot*, Chatto & Windus, London, 1961. A valuable study of George Eliot's artistry, especially notable for its clear and careful presentation of issues.

LERNER, LAURENCE, and HOLSTROM, JOHN, *George Eliot and Her Readers*, Bodley Head, London, 1966. A representative collection of contemporary reviews.

STEPHEN, LESLIE, *George Eliot*, Duckworth, London, 1919. An early and influential biographical and critical study, readable and lively, if somewhat dated.

THALE, JEROME, *The Novels of George Eliot*, Columbia University Press, New York, 1959. An interesting introduction, less polished in style and crisp in procedure than that of Bennett, above. Also deals with individual novels.

C. *Articles and Parts of Books*. I have listed only articles not available in Haight, *A Century of George Eliot Criticism*, above.

COLBY, ROBERT A., *Fiction With a Purpose*, Indiana University Press, 1967. Contains studies of *The Mill on the Floss* and *Middlemarch* in relation to Victorian culture.

KERMODE, FRANK, 'Lawrence and the Apocalyptic Types', *Critical Quarterly*, Spring and Summer, 1968, 14-38. A difficult but rewarding study of *Middlemarch* and D. H. Lawrence's *Women in Love*.

KNOEPFLMACHER, U. C., *Religious Humanism and the Victorian Novel*, Princeton, 1965. Studies several writers, including George Eliot, in the context of Victorian ideas.

LEAVIS, F. R., *The Great Tradition*, Chatto & Windus, London, 1948. The section on George Eliot can be fairly said to have initiated modern criticism of the author.

PREYER, ROBERT, 'Beyond the Liberal Imagination: Vision and Unreality in *Daniel Deronda*', *Victorian Studies*, September 1960, 33-54. A seminal article.

115

VAN GHENT, DOROTHY, *The English Novel: Form and Function*, Rinehart, New York, 1953. Contains an important essay on *Adam Bede*.

2, 38